FOR HUFF 1760

GARRY HUFF

FORT HUFF, 1760

GARRY HUFF

CITI OF
BOOKS

CITIOFBOOKS, INC.
3736 Eubank NE Suite A1
Albuquerque, NM 87111-3579
www.citiofbooks.com
Hotline: 1 (877) 389-2759
Fax: 1 (505) 930-7244

Ordering Information:
Quantity sales. Special discounts are available on quantity purchases by corporations, associations, and others. For details, contact the publisher at the address above.

Printed in the United States of America.
ISBN-13:   Paperback   979-8-89391-491-7
              eBook   979-8-89391-493-1
              Hardback   979-8-89391-492-4

Library of Congress Control Number: 2024926810

Content

Introduction

Adam Huff in 1760 came to Kentucky in a covered wagon, bringing with him his family; Ruth his wife, his 19-year old son John, and his16-year old son James. Also, a Slave by the name of George and his family came, Liz his wife and Emma his daughter. There were at least 20 people of varying degree of kin in the seven wagons that followed. Talking Bear was high chief to the ve tribes of the Cherokee nation. Two Stars, the Chief's sister, had been the only mother Talking Bear had ever known. Red Hawk was Talking Bear's top brave whose friendship would be tested to the limits. Little Dove was Two Starz's sister in spirit seeing as how they both had to play mother to their little brothers instead of being just girls. Emma was the slave girl who lost her heart as well as her sight for her love for Red Hawk. Rose Marie, the seven-year old who was the only one left once the fever struck the wagon train. Gray Wolf could not let his love be known for Little Dove because of his hate for Red Hawk.

Adam pulled back hard on the lead rains to stop all four horses that pulled his wagon from West Virginia. He had timed it so the horses were standing in water over their feet. Adam thought that by doing it this way all four horses could drink their fill. Adam's bright blue eyes squinted as they scanned the mountain that lye before him. This must be it; Adam thought as he climbed down from the wagon carrying a rolled up beaver pelt. Adam unrolled the beaver pelt that had been used as a map to a mountain, according to the map all the land at the foot of the mountain was what the deed called for. The map showed two creeks; one going down each side of the mountain separating the flat lands from the mountain, according to Dan Gains-the mountain man who had sold Adam the map. He had also told Adam that there was a log cabin that went with the deal. According to the story, Gains had been given the land by the Indians for saving the son of a Chief. All Adam had to do was show the chief the pelt and the Indians wouldn't give him any trouble after that. People started to gather around Adam.

"Is this where we'll stay the night?" John asked as he came up behind Adam.

"Right son, this is the place we have been looking for." Adam said before falling quiet.

"This place will be ours forever and no one will ever take our land again." Adam told John.

People started climbing down from their wagons and coming toward them.

"Why have we stopped?" They started asking.

"This is it!" John yelled out with excitement that soon spread to the rest of the people.

Adam hadn't noticed the dark black rain cloud over head until it blacked out the sun.

"Everyone back on the wagons." Adam cried.

Panic replaced the feeling of joy everyone was feeling in fear they were being attacked.

"Up there!" Adam said pointing at large hill by the tree line.

The hill was just big enough that all six wagons would fit on it tightly. Once it started raining the creek bed quickly filled and water spilled over its banks. It did not take long until the spot Adam had chosen was the only one not under water. Adam stood and looked out at the bottom land under water.

"How often do you think that happens, pa?" John asked as he came up behind Adam.

"I hope we just got here on a bad day." Adam said turning to look at John.

John could hear the fear in Adam's voice and then he saw what Adam had been looking at.

"Tomorrow I want you and James to go find that cabin that is around here somewhere." Adam said.

"What are you going to do pa?" John asked as they walked back into the camp.

"I'm going to take George and try and find the Indians before they find us." Adam replied.

"Think them Indians will leave us alone, Master Adam?" George asked as the two joined him by the fire.

George was just a few years younger than Adam. Adam's father had given George to him as a boy. In fact, George was the first slave Adam had ever owned. George had been with Adam so long now he is like family and is treated with respect. After seeing how other slaves were treated on the plantation George felt lucky to belong to Adam.

"I think they will wait till tomorrow at least." Adam said as he sat down. All three men began looking at the black outline of the mountain behind them. Emma called out that supper was ready to eat so all three men headed toward the campfire. Emma was George and Liz's daughter and since Adam never had a girl child he loved her like she was the daughter he never had. Both boys loved her like a sister instead of a slave.

The rain stopped sometime during the night and by the next morning the water was going down. The camp was east of the mountain so when the sun came up the mountain cast its shadow on it. As soon as John got up he went looking for the place James had spent the night.

John found James wide awake and setting by the cook fire with Emma. "Master James, you knows all them things you been saying about them Indians isn't true." Emma was saying as John reached them.

James was three years younger than John and thought he was ready to take on the world at sixteen.

"Master John tells Master James that Pa said the Indians are not going to hurt us?" Emma asked.

"Girl, you got things to do, don't you?" John asked before turning to James.

"And you are going with me." John said roughly to James.

"You have better things to do besides making Emma more frightened than she already is." John added.

James knew from the tone of John's voice that he was in no mood for his foolishness. George had gotten caught up in James's story as well.

"Is what the boy saying true Master John?" George asked as he got to his feet as well.

John first looked at Emma then at George.

"Emma you stay in camp and help your mom." John told her as the three turned and walked away.

"Where is the cabin to be at?" James asked as they walked.

"I don't know yet but we must find it so we can get things ready by winter." John replied.

"Is I going with you Master John?" George asked.

John stopped and turned to George.

"No George, you and Pa are going to find the Indians." John told George. The expression on George's face told John that George didn't like that idea at all. If hiding from the Indians was not enough now he was looking for them.

As soon as the men reached Adam's wagon he was standing at the back taking out the guns.

"Here." Adam said and he handed John a gun.

"I'm only going to say this once." Adam added. "Do not shoot this unless your life depends on it. If you were to kill an Indian they would come here and kill us all. Do you understand?" Adam asked.

"Yes Pa, I understand." John said as he took the gun.

"Where is mine?" James asked holding out his hand.

Adam looked at James for a few seconds before he said anything.

"You had better leave it here." Adam said.

"You let me hunt with it pa." James said still holding out his hand.

"He could get some game while we are out pa." John told Adam.

"Do not shoot this unless there is fresh game on the other end." Adam told James as he handed him a gun.

"Ok pa. I won't." James said as he took the gun.

After going what John thought was the right distance he stopped to check the map. While John looked at the pelt and tried to see where they were James went around him. James decided to go ahead and see what was there so he walked on. James thought he heard something so he stopped behind a tree and peeked out. There standing getting his morning drink of water was a large white tail buck. James became so excited that when he tried to get the gun up to shoot the deer it caught on a bush and went off. It was not until then that James saw the Indian on the other side of the creek. The Indian wore a vest made of bone crowned with three red feathers.

"Wait! Stop!" James shouted as the brave ran into the woods. As James watched the Indian vanish into the woods he realized that the Indian was yelling a war cry.

"Come back." James called hopelessly.

The sound of gunfire brought John to James fast.

"What is going on?" John asked even before he reached James.

"Indian." James said pointing at where the brave entered the woods.

John couldn't believe what he was hearing. Did his little brother just get them all killed.

"Are you crazy?!" John screamed in anger. "You can't go around shooting at the Indians James."

"I didn't shoot at him, I didn't even see him until the buck ran off." James said in a frightened voice.

"What did the Indian look like?" John asked.

"You know an Indian; he wore a vest made of some kind of bone with red feathers on it. Do you think he was a chief or something?" James asked.

"Chief or not you can bet he will be coming back with a lot more of his friends." John said.

John could see nothing but trees in front of them knowing the Indians were out there somewhere.

Adam's bright blue eyes were squinted almost shut as he scanned for the slightest movement. The sun had been up for over an hour and Adam was sure that if they were coming they would be here by now. Just as Adam was about to quit looking he saw someone coming his way.

"Is it an Indian Master Adam?" George asked.

"Don't know yet." Adam said as they waited for the man to get closer.

"Must be a trapper." Adam told George when the man got close enough to see he was leading a mule.

"Just because he is white you keep an eye on him George." Adam said.

"Morning Mister." The old trapper said as he got down off his horse and dropped the lead rains to the mule.

Adam waited for the trapper to say what he wanted before he spoke.

"The name is Adam Gains." The old man said and stuck out his hand.

"Adam Huff." Adam said as he shook the hand.

The trapper's eyes were on the wagons as he shook Adam's hand. All these wagons had bound to have gotten Talking Bear to notice by now Gains thought.

"Want a cup of coffee?" Adam asked as he invited Gains to sit down.

"Do you think that he went back to the village?" James asked just above a whisper.

"Yes and if he was the Chief it was to get his braves and come back." John said as he kept on walking. "If he thinks you were trying to kill him he will kill us all no matter what this thing says." John said as he held up the beaver pelt.

It soon became clear that the Indian didn't have to go very far to catch up to his friends. John couldn't see them but he could feel them and they were close. John knew he and James were being hoarded back toward camp on both sides of the creek. John felt like he was being pushed so all of them would be together when the Indians struck. It was like being stocked by wolves.

"Should we cut through the woods?" James asked as John sped up their pace.

"No. Just keep walking; we don't know how many are in these woods. They haven't shot at us yet so they don't want us dead." John said as he quickened his pace even more.

"When we make it back to camp I'll never leave it again." James said as he followed John's pace.

The words no sooner than left James's lips when he saw Talking Bear and Red Hawk come into view.

James stopped and yelled, "There he is!" while pointing at Red Hawk. When John stopped and looked at what James was talking about he saw them too. John could also tell that the one James pointed at was not the chief. The chief sat his horse like a king and his braves that sat beside him treated him like one. Talking Bear left no question as to who held the power around here. Then he saw Red Hawk and the red feathers.

Adam was trying to explain to Gains about the deed on a pelt that brought them here. Adam Gains burst out in a laugh that shook his whole body.

"That so called deed you say you have is not a land deed Mr. Huff. It's a diary." Gains was able to say once he stopped laughing.

"A what?" Adam Huff asked not knowing if he had heard Gains right.

"A gift from a chief for the man who married his daughter; it's not a land deed."

Seeing that Huff still didn't understand Gains tried to explain it more.

"It means that the whole village will treat the man holding it like one of the village." Gains said. Where is the pelt?" Gains asked.

"My son John has it now looking for a cabin that the deed said was around here." Adam said.

Adam saw the smile leave Gains's face and a look of shock replace it.

"It's a wedding license Mr. Huff." Gains told Adam. "It means that anyone who hands it to the chief will marry his daughter." Gains went on to say.

"What about the cabin?" Adam Huff asked not paying any mind to what Gains was trying to tell him.

"The only way you could live in that cabin is if you married the chief's sister!" Gains roared loudly.

"I thought you said the chief's daughter?" Adam Huff asked now more confused than ever.

"The man you got that pelt off of is my brother Dan Gains." Adam Gains said staring at Adam.

"He was married to Two Stars the sister of Talking Bear, the chief now. His father was Iron Bear, the chief of the whole Cherokee nation around here." Gains said.

"He gave Two Stars to my brother, Dan, for saving the life of Talking Bear when he was a boy.

To these Indians here the life of a chief is the most important thing to the village." Gains said.

"Two Stars hasn't lived in the house since my brother left ten years ago. I can tell you right now Huff; she isn't going to like the idea of being your wife." Gains said with a big laugh.

Both John and James were never gladder to see a place as they were to see the camp come into view. The two boys were almost running by the time they reached the camp. Adam Gains saw the two boys first running as hard as they could toward the wagons. Adam Huff started walking out to meet them when Gains grabbed him by the arm. Just as Adam was about to ask him what he was doing, he too saw the Indians come into view.

"That Mr. Huff is Talking Bear, chief of the Cherokee nation." Gains said pointing at him.

"At least he isn't wearing war paint." Gains said as he lowered his arm.

"Can you speak their tongue?" Adam Huff asked Gains knowing he couldn't speak a word of it himself.

"It wasn't my fault pa." James was saying even before he stopped running. "What is he talking about John?" Adam asked.

"He was shooting at a deer and the gun went off accidently. There was an Indian on the other side of the creek and he may think James was shooting at him."

"Should I go get the Guns Master?" George asked.

"No George. Not yet." Adam said as he watched the three Indians stop just outside the camp.

"Put all the guns on the ground while I go and try to explain that it was just an accident." Adam said.

Gains had already gone out to talk to Talking Bear while Adam was talking to the boys.

As Gains talked he kept pointing at Adam and the boys. John stopped Adam this time as he saw Gains coming back toward them. Gains looked back over his shoulder as he made his way back into the camp.

"Pa, what are they going to do?" James asked as Gains got closer.

"I don't know son." Adam said just as Mr. Gains reached them.

Adam Gains stopped right in front of the two men and boys before he began to talk. Gains was looking at the boys but talking to Adam as he spoke.

"Talking Bear said that your boys were shooting at Red Hawk down by the creek. Is that true?" Gains asked.

"It was an accident!" Adam said loudly. "The boy wasn't shooting at the Indian. The gun just went off can't you explain that to them?" Adam asked Gains.

"You don't need me to tell Talking Bear anything. He can speak English as good as you and me. You see when my brother saved Talking Bear's life he kept following Dan around every day. He soon learned how to speak English as good as a white man. Once he learned he taught it to most of the village." Gains told Adam.

Gains let out a little laugh then said, "That's how he got his name Talking Bear."

Adam's eyes never left Talking Bear as he slowly made his way toward him.

Red Hawk stood at Talking Bear's right and Gray Wolf on his left. Both warriors had an arrow in their bow with the string pulled tight. Adam walked slowly toward the three Indians not knowing what was going to happen once he got there. Adam could hear his own heart beat and the closer he got to Talking Bear the louder it got.

"It was all just a miss understanding." Adam said as he reached out his hand.

"The boy wasn't shooting at your warrior. The gun got caught on a bush and went off."

Without a word just the movement of Talking Bear's arm the two braves lowered their bows.

Adam didn't believe how right Gains was until he heard Talking Bear speak.

"Who was the boy shooting at, if he wasn't shooting at my warrior?" Talking Bear asked pointing at Red Hawk.

"He was trying to shoot a deer the boy didn't know that the brave was there until the gun went off." Adam told the Chief.

"Was there a deer there?" Talking Bear asked as he turned to Red Hawk.

"Yes, I saw the deer there as well." Red hawk said as his eyes fell on Adam.

"What are you doing here?" Talking Bear asked Adam in an angry voice as he turned to Adam.

"Well you see I bought this land deed from Dan Gains the man who saved you." Adam said hoping that was all he had to do.

Talking Bear looked puzzled as he tried to understand what this white man was saying.

"We are Indian. We do not think that land is owned by anyone. The land belongs to all.

We'll never give our land to you or anyone else." Talking Bear said angrily. "What about the deed?" Adam asked.

"The man that sold you the land robbed you. My people didn't." Talking Bear said.

"What about the beaver pelt with the cabin on it?" Adam asked. Adam could see the expression change on Talking Bear's face when he said cabin.

"You all will have to go. You are not wanted here." Talking Bear said pointing in the direction the wagons had come.

"Chief it has took us six weeks to get here we have used up most of our supplies. We couldn't go back right now even if we wanted to." Adam told Talking Bear loudly.

Adam could tell that Talking Bear knew what he was talking about when he said pelt.

"Where is this pelt you speak of?" Talking Bear asked.

"My son has it. That was what they were doing when all this happened. I'll go get it." Adam said as he headed back to camp.

John saw Adam wave his arm telling him to come to him. John left James and George standing with Gains as he headed toward Adam and the Indians. John still carried the beaver pelt with him as he met Adam coming to him. Everyone in camp began to gather where George and James stood with Gains. They all watched as Adam turned and walked back to the Chief and the braves with John.

"I saw this one looking at something just before the other one shot at me." Red Hawk said angrily.

"Show the Chief the pelt boy and hurry up." Adam said in a rigorous voice.

John could hear the fear in his pa's voice. Everyone began to gather where George, John, and Gains stood watching. John reached out his hand holding the beaver pelt and gave it to Talking Bear. As soon as Gains saw what John was handing Talking Bear he realized that he had forgot one important thing. He had not told Adam that whoever handed Talking Bear the pelt had just married Two Stars. Gains began running toward Adam waving his arms yelling stop as loud as he could. John noticed the look on the chief's face as he gave Talking Bear the pelt.

Gains was to late the boy had just married Two Stars the chief's sister.

"See I told you Chief we had a deed." Adam said with a smile.

Once Gains reached them he could tell by the expression on Talking Bear's face that he didn't like the idea either. Talking Bear knew the true meaning of the pelt. He watched as Iron Bear gave it to Gains. The pelt wasn't a land deed at all it was a marriage licenses for his sister.

"Your boy has just married Two Stars and from the look on Talking Bear's face he doesn't care for her new husband." Gains said once he caught his breath.

The way Two Stars got her name, her father had seen two shooting stars close together. Talking Bear knew how Two Stars had felt about Dan Gains. Talking Bear didn't like the idea that he was the one who had to tell her she was now married to a young boy. A young white boy. Talking Bear wasn't the only one that didn't like what was going on. Red Hawk was looking at John and shaking his head, he had come here to kill the whites and now he had to accept one as a brother. Surely Talking Bear wasn't going to go through with this marriage Red Hawk thought. Talking Bear turned and looked at the braves behind him.

Talking Bear knew that to not honor Iron Bear's word the word of a chief would dishonor the whole village.

"My people will honor my father's word." He said as he turned and walked back to his horse.

"There will be a brave bring a horse later on." The Chief said as he led the Indians away.

A smile came to Adam's face as he watched the Chief ride away. As Gains and John started back toward camp, Adam stood watching the Indians leaving.

"Does this mean the land is ours?" John asked as the two walked back. "No boy. It just means you are now a married man." Gains said as he walked and shook his head. "You have no idea what you just did, do you?" Gains asked once they reached the camp.

"It means from now on the Indians will leave us alone doesn't it?" John asked.

"It means the Indians will leave you alone but it doesn't mean a thing for the rest of the people." Gains told John.

Two Stars sat in her teepee talking to Little Dove her closest friend since childhood.

Talking Bear walked in looked at Little Dove and said, "Go." Then stood and waited for her to leave.

A cold feeling slowly made its way up Two Starz's neck making the hair stand on end.

"What is it brother?" She asked as she got to her feet.

Talking Bear waited until Little Dove had left before he said anything.

"You have a new husband." He said then fell silent and just stared at her.

"My husband, as you called him, has been gone for over three years. He will never be back." Two Stars said with fear in her voice.

"This time it's not Dan Gains. It's a boy; a white boy." Talking Bear said shaking his head.

"I won't do it Talking Bear. I will not go back to that cabin again!" Two Stars yelled.

"The boy has the pelt. There is nothing I can do but go by tribal law!" Talking Bear yelled back. "You will go back to the cabin." Talking Bear said.

Two Stars said nothing more as Talking Bear turned and walked out. Two Stars felt weak in her knees as she sat back down. Her mind began to filll with thoughts of what it had been like when she lived in the cabin with Dan. She had been only fifthteen when her father had given her to Dan Gains.

"I'll never go to that cabin again. I will not be given to another man just because of a beaver pelt. He isn't even a man yet." She told herself as she shook her head.

Two Stars knew what she was going to do, she would have Talking Bear kill the boy. Two Stars could tell that Talking Bear didn't like the idea either so she would have the boy killed. Just as Two Stars started out the door she got a new idea. It wouldn't hurt to go check out this boy before she had him killed.

"I'll hide until the boy shows up."

"If I don't like what I see then I would have him fed to the bears."

Two Stars looked herself over as she headed toward the cabin. She found the cabin just the way she had left it three years ago. If it wasn't for the dust and spider webs everything was where she had left it. As Two Starz's eyes scanned the room her eyes locked on the handmade bed setting in the corner. She remembered it being there the first night Dan brought her there. She also remembered how badly Dan had treated her from then on. The only thing that Two Stars regretted about the day Dan had left was that he had not given her the baby she had longed for. Two Stars thought for a minute of how besides her and Little Dove the rest of the squaws had at least one by now. Two Stars didn't know if it was because of Dan's age or what for why she had none. The idea that she was still young enough to have children drove her on. At the age of twenty three she still had a chance Two Stars told herself as she made her way into the woods behind a hill. Two Stars placed herself to where the afternoon sun would be in the boy's face as he approached.

"What do you mean; do I know what will be expected of me on a wedding night?" John asked angrily.

"I'm not going through with this marriage; I'm going to tell her that it's all just a mistake. I can't marry some girl I don't know. Let alone love!" John shouted.

"What do you mean you're not going through with it?" Gains asked this time he wasn't laughing. "I can tell you now if you don't go through with it you will insult the whole village. If you do that, not a single one of you will live to see another sunset!" Gains yelled loudly.

John didn't like the idea of getting married but the thought of not seeing another sunset he liked even less.

"What are you going to do John?" Adam asked. "Ok. I'll go to the cabin and try to explain to this Two Stars that it was just a mistake." John said.

"Good I'll get everyone to load up the wagons so we can go to the cabin." Adam was smiling as he started walking off.

"What do you mean get everyone ready to go?!" Gains yelled.

"Go where?" Gains asked.

"Well to the cabin of course." Adam told Gains once Gains released his arm again.

"Now look Huff, the only one that's going to the cabin is your son. Two Stars is marring your son not everyone in this camp." Gains said angrily pointing at John.

"Where are we supposed to live?" Adam asked.

"Mr. Huff, It's going to be up to Two Stars if you live at all."

Adam fell silent as his mind tried to absorb what he had just heard.

"Huff, if I were you I'd keep your people away from the Indians." Gains said as he mounted his horse.

Once he made himself comfortable Gains turned to Adam, "if you don't they will get you all killed."

Gains rode off without looking back over his shoulder. Adam and John watched Gains until he was out of sight then turned and stared at each other. Neither John nor Adam could believe what they had just heard. Adam knew that the people now coming toward him were going to ask questions he couldn't answer.

"Master Adam, what them Indians say?" George asked. Just as Adam had predicted everyone began shouting their questions at John and him as they made it back to camp. Even though Ruth and Liz hadn't reached Adam yet he could see the fear on Ruth's face.

"Ruth I'm afraid. I really messed up things this time." Adam said as Ruth finally reached him.

Adam watched as the look of fear took the place of the smile Ruth wore. "I may have put us all in danger." Adam was saying just before falling silent. "Our son John is now a married man and he had no choice about it either." Adam said as he hugged Ruth. "This so called deed is a marriage license and not a land deed." Adam said as he shook the pelt at the people.

"John is still too young to be getting married." Ruth was saying as she took John's hand in hers.

"Believe me maw, you wouldn't like the other way out of this." John said as he released Ruth's hand.

Liz and Emma stood behind George and while Liz stood in silence Emma kept asking George "What's going on pa?"

"Be quite girl and I might find out!" George yelled at Emma over his shoulder.

Everyone began yelling for Adam to tell them what was going on. "What was he going to tell them?" Adam asked himself as he looked for an answer.

Two Stars soon grew tired of waiting for the boy to show up. She decided that she would wait for him in the cabin and left her hiding place. Two Starz's eyes locked on the handmade bed, the set Dan had brought her that first night. She remembered how Little Dove had told her that it would hurt the first time but it would get better with a smile. It was about the only time that Dan was kind to her she thought to herself.

"There they are." Two Stars said as she saw the two water buckets setting in the corner.

Two Stars walked over and picked up the buckets then headed out the door to fill them. She had found out a long time ago that the best way she could get her mind off Dan was to clean the house. As Two Stars began to clean her thoughts went back to that boy now coming to claim her as his wife.

"What was this boy going to expect from me?" She kept asking herself.

At sundown Red Hawk came to camp leading a white horse.

"I think the horse is for you." Adam said as Red Hawk stopped right in front of John. Without a word John glanced at Adam then climbed on the horse and let Red Hawk lead him away.

"Adam you have got to stop him." Ruth said as she hurried to catch John before he left.

Adam caught Ruth by the arms and turned her to face him. "You have got to let him go Ruth, if we don't do what the Indians want they will kill us. Don't you understand?!" Adam yelled.

Ruth brought her hands to her eyes and wiped the tears that blurred her last look at her son.

"He will be alright Ruth." Adam said as the two watched John and the Indian ride from sight.

John tried talking to Red Hawk as they rode but Red Hawk faced forward without saying a word.

John didn't know if the Indian's silence was because he didn't know English or it was part of the ceremony.

"This is where Two Stars will be." Red Hawk said as he dropped the lead rains and pointed to a cabin.

The cabin sat on a bluff high above the creek bed back among the trees. Red Hawk waited for John to get off the horse to hand him back the rope before he headed back to the village. Once John reached the cabin he could tell that it had been a while since anyone had lived here. John's eyes stayed locked on the cabin door as he slowly made his way to it. The sound of someone walking on the porch caused Two Stars to glance up as John stepped through the front door. She rose to her feet and stood there in silence as John came in. He was tall with black hair and a muscular body for a boy of his age. John's eyes scanned the room then locked on the bed that sat in the corner. John hadn't quite known what to expect when he got there but a women as pretty as her wasn't it.

It was like time had been turned back for Two Stars as she watched John stare at the bed.

The boy she saw standing before her was not much older than she was the first time she saw that bed.

"My name is John." he said as he reached out his hand to Two Stars.

"I thought you would be older." Two Stars said without taking John's hand.

"I thought you would be much older too." John said as he let his arm drop back to his side.

John stood in silence as Two Starz's eyes looked him over as though she was buying a horse. Two Stars thought to herself that if she wanted to know if it was her or Dan that couldn't have kids, this young boy would be able to tell her.

"Let me explain." John said as he held up the pelt.

"This is what a mountain man sold to my pa as a land deed; we didn't know it was a marriage license. I'm sure you don't like this idea no more than I do." John said in an unconvincing voice. "If you want we can call this whole thing off."

John saw anger flash in Two Starz's dark eyes.

"I am a gift from my people for saving the life of a tribal Chief. Would you dare insult the village by refusing?" Two Stars asked.

"No I just thought you would want an older man is all." John said trying to sooth Two Starz's anger. "I meant no disrespect to you or your people." John told her.

"It is I who will decide if you are to become my husband or not!" Two Stars said angrily. "You will sleep there." She said pointing at a bear skin she had placed in the corner for him.

Two Stars noticed how John's eyes went from where she was pointing to the bed across the room.

"You make a fire and I'll fix us something to eat." Two Stars said as she watched John stare at the bed. A smile came to Two Starz's face as she remembered how she had done the same thing the first time she had saw that bed.

"What were you saying about a fire?" John asked.

"A fire to cook something to eat and keep us warm through the night." John noticed a hint of anger return in Two Starz's voice for having to tell John twice. Two Starz's dark eyes watched as John went about building the fire. The heat felt good in just a few minutes so John walked over to where he was to sleep and sat down on the bear skin. A cloud of dust rose in the air all around him so John was waving his arm trying to brush it away. John wondered if it was because he was young or that every man felt awkward on their first night. Two Stars almost laughed out loud but was able to catch herself and only smiled.

"As you can see it's been three years since anyone has been here." she said.

"I see." John said after he stopped waving his arm and watched the dust make its way back to the floor.

Two Stars went quickly to the fire place and knelt down so John couldn't see her smile.

Ruth watched how the light from the campfire reflected off Adam's face. She could tell that his mind was thinking of his oldest son out there in the darkness somewhere. As Ruth watched him she knew that Adam wasn't only worried for John but for the rest of the people as well.

"Do you think the Indians will hurt John?" Ruth asked.

Adam tried to get the doubt out of his eyes before he answered her.

"Ruth, I'll bet the boy is having the best time of his life. You remember how it was for us don't you?" Adam asked.

Adam could tell that Ruth did remember by the way a smile crossed her face. The sound of George coming to them in a hurry drew both

Adam's and Ruth's attention.

"Have you seen Emma?" He asked once he caught his breath. "No I haven't seen her." Adam said as he got to his feet.

"Liz said she thought she could be down at the creek fetching water to wash her hair."

"Doesn't the girl know that no one was to leave this camp this late?!" Adam yelled once he got to his feet.

"Yes Master. I done told the girl that but I can't find her anywhere." George said.

"I'll help you find her." Adam told George as the two men walked toward the creek.

The sun was just falling behind the mountain as Talking Bear made his way to where he had sent Red Hawk to watch the white's. Talking Bear was having trouble deciding what he was going to do about the settlers. Every fiber of him told him to kill them instead of driving them out. There was nothing he could do about the boy that was now married to his sister. That left him with twenty other white's to think about. The idea of the white man coming here and polluting his blood angered Talking Bear. Red Hawk kept his eyes on the camp. Talking Bear saw Red Hawk lying face down under a dead tree. From his view point they could see anything that went on in camp as well as the creek.

"What are they doing?" Talking Bear asked as he lied down beside Red Hawk.

"I think they are getting ready to lie down for the night." Red Hawk said without looking back. "The only one that's come out of camp is that girl by the water." Red Hawk said.

Red Hawk didn't know if it was the falling sun or the darkness but there was something different about the girl.

"You see anything strange about that girl?" Red Hawk asked.

Talking Bear looked at the girl but saw nothing different about her.

"No she looks just like the rest." Talking Bear told him.

"Maybe it's just me being tired. You know it's been a long day." Red Hawk said.

"I'll send Gray Wolf to relieve you." Talking Bear said as he prepared to leave.

Emma kept her eyes staring into the darkness as she dipped the bucket into the water.

"You want me to catch her?" Red Hawk asked.

"No. We want these people to leave our land and not come back." Talking Bear said as he too watched Emma. "If we take one of their women every man in that camp would come after her. We don't want a war with these people we just want them gone." Talking Bear told Red Hawk. "Come let's go back to the village." Talking Bear said as he headed for the horses.

Red Hawk kept his eyes on Emma as he walked behind Talking Bear into the darkness.

A large frog crocked loudly close to where Emma drew the water. The sound frightened her so much that she spilled most of the water she had just drew from the creek. The camp seemed so far away now that Emma was frightened. Emma ran as fast as she could for the safety of the camp not caring how much water was lost.

Adam and George met Emma just as she reached the wagons.

"Where you been girl?" George asked as he grabbed Emma by the arm.

"I was just getting water pa." Emma said as she wiped tears from her eyes. The fear of what George was going to do to her was just as great as the fear she had of the Indians.

"You stupid girl, Do you know what them Indians would do to you if they took you?"

Emma could hear the fear along with anger in George's voice as he slapped her. Emma dropped the bucket spilling what water had made it to camp.

"If the Indians had taken you we all could have been killed trying to get you back!" Adam yelled.

Adam stood staring into the darkness shaking his head. Adam knew that he was going to have to make a decision on leaving or staying to fight for the land. Adam knew that if they left he would go without his son John. Adam remembered seeing at least fifty braves that morning with Talking Bear. Adam remembered thinking that there could be two hundred more in them trees out there.

"I'm not going anywhere without my boy no matter what the others do." He said in a low voice.

"You need to take the strap to that girl, George." Adam said as George and Emma turned to go.

"Yes, Master Adam. I do that as soon as I get her back to the wagon." George told him.

"You going to get a whipin girl." George said as he pushed Emma ahead of him.

George and Emma were out of sight by the time Adam came back into camp. James caught Adam just as he entered the camp.

"Pa, have you found Emma yet?" James asked.

"Yes boy. She is with George now he promised to give her a good whipping." Adam told James.

James looked in the direction he knew George had taken her before he spoke.

"Pa, you know that Emma didn't mean no harm she just wasn't thinking?" James said.

"Thinking like that will kill us all." Adam said.

As John sat across from Two Stars eating the food she had fixed not a word was spoken.

It was John who broke the silence.

"If your people don't believe in owning land what was the pelt all about?" He asked.

Two Stars stared at John for a minute before she said anything.

"The pelt shows that whoever holds it will be treated as part of the village." Two Stars paused before she went on. "Whoever holds it owns me and this cabin" She said weaving her arm through the air. I may have said too much already Two Stars told herself then fell quiet once more.

John thought of what Two Stars had just said then spoke.

"Then if I don't own the land, I own you and this cabin." John said while mockingly waving his arm.

Two Stars shot to her feet and yelled at John.

"No one will ever own me again! If you try I'll have you tied to a horse and dragged to death. Do you understand?!" She yelled. As he looked in her eyes he knew she meant it.

Two Stars thought she had pressed her luck too far when John jumped to his feet.

"Look lady, I'm here for my people just like you. The only reason we came here in the first place is because the English king took our land. Pa bought the pelt thinking we at last had land we could call our own." John said loudly.

"My brother will make your people leave here or he will kill them." Two Stars said just as loud. "The only one the pelt will protect is you not your people." Two Stars told John.

"Is Talking Bear going to attack the wagons?" John asked with fear in his voice.

"I don't know." Two Stars said as she looked away.

"If they leave and don't come back. Talking Bear won't hurt anyone I'm sure." Two Stars said. "We don't own this mountain but just like you we won't let you whites take our home either."

"What about me?" John asked.

"You can go with them if that's what you want to do." Two Stars said in a voice so low that John could barely hear her. "It's time to sleep." She said pointing at the corner.

Talking Bear tossed a stick of wood into the fire and watched the sparks climb their way from view. Tomorrow he would demand for the whites to leave his mountain. From the time Dan Gains shot that bear Talking Bear new of the white man's power. Talking Bear respected that power and feared it. The Shawnee were his mortal enemy and were attacking his villages to the south. With each raid they would come closer to his village. If it wasn't for needing every brave in the village he would kill every white man and women there. The other whites would be afraid to come there then, Talking Bear told himself. The sound coming from where Standing Bird was sleeping with the girls caught his attention. What I wouldn't give to be able to sleep like that he thought.

Sleep didn't come easy for anyone on the mountain that night. It seemed that everyone knew that tomorrow was going to be a day none of them would ever forget. Was it her dream and the morning sun coming through the window that woke Two Stars? She wasn't sure which so she quietly got to her feet. Two Stars placed her eyes on John as she made her way to the table to sit down. He looked so peaceful sleeping on the bear skin in the corner across the room. Two Stars noticed something outside that drew her attention from John. When she got up to see what it was she became frightened. Two Stars let out a cry when she saw a Shawnee brave standing just outside the door. The sound woke John from his sleep leaving him not knowing the cause. Once John got his eyes open he saw Two Stars staring out the window. John could tell from the look on her face she was frightened. John got to his feet as quickly as he could and rushed to Two Starz's side. When John saw the Indian he thought it was one of the braves from the village.

"What is that on his face?" John asked.

"War paint." Two Stars said as quietly as she could. "Has Talking Bear started already?" John asked.

"He is not from our village. He is a Shawnee." Two Stars told John. "What kind of warrior had I got?" Two Stars asked herself. This boy doesn't even know a Shawnee from her own people.

"Who is he at war with?" John asked in a very calm voice. "He is here to kill your people and mine." Two Stars said as she backed away from the window.

It was about that time the brave turned and looked at John staring at him. The brave kicked the door open and came through it. Seeing that John was unarmed a smile came to his face. The door slammed so hard against the cabin wall that it shook the whole cabin. Two Stars was just out of reach of the door or it would have hurt her badly.

"Come on you bastard!" John yelled inviting the brave to come and get him. When the brave saw that John's gun was across the room he pulled his knife and started toward John. John watched the smile leave the brave's face as Two Stars plunged her knife into the brave's back. The brave was dead before he hit the floor; he hit the floor with a thump.

Adam had seen the brave enter the cabin so he increased his pace to it. "He is not here alone." Two Stars said as she heard Adam come onto the porch.

John watched as she drew back the bloody knife to through it at whoever came through that door.

"Wait Two Stars." John said as he grabbed her arm that held the knife. John stepped between Adam and Two Stars. "This is my pa." John said as he let go of Two Starz's arm. "He won't hurt you."

"You can bet that he wasn't alone." Two Stars said as she lowered the knife. "We should go back to the wagons and warn them." Adam told them. Two Stars showed she agreed by a shake of her head. All three followed the creek bed knowing that it was the fastest way back. Adam saw that they knew about the Indians by the way every wagon had at least one gun sticking out of it. Two Stars had to admit the sight of all them guns frightened her even if they were on her side. She found that she was more frightened of the guns than she was of the brave she just killed.

"It's ok." John said when Two Stars stopped in her tracks just outside the wagons.

Two Stars looked into John's eyes and without another word entered the camp.

It seemed that everyone was looking at her as she went in.

Talking Bear got to his feet and headed outside when he heard Gray Wolf call his name.

When Talking Bear reached the door he saw Gray Wolf sitting on his horse and a dead Shawnee brave lying at his feet.

"Where did you kill him?" Talking Bear asked as he looked the brave over.

Talking Bear saw that the dead brave was stabbed in his back.

"Where did you kill him?" Talking Bear asked again.

"I didn't kill him. I found him in the cabin and no one else." Gray Wolf told him. "Two Stars and the boy must have gone to the white man's camp." Gray Wolf said as both he and Talking Bear looked in that direction.

In just a few minutes every brave in the village was on horseback and headed toward the wagons and the white men who lived there. A Shawnee war party had followed Adam and John as they left the cabin. Not knowing that the wagons were well armed The Shawnee braves came straight in to death. Adam had everyone hold their fire and let the braves come close before they fired their guns. Talking Bear and his braves reached the camp just as the first volley was fired.

Talking Bear saw the look on Snow beaver's face, the young brave who wanted to attack the whites yesterday. Pure shock was all Talking Bear saw as he watched the Shawnee braves die.

"Yesterday you wanted to do the same wasn't you?" Talking Bear asked. There were five Shawnee braves that turned back after seeing all the other braves drop to the ground. To their surprise they turned straight into Talking Bear and his braves. Three of the remaining Shawnee braves were killed right off.

"Keep the other two alive and make them talk before they die." Talking Bear ordered.

Both Red Hawk and Gray Wolf started to follow Talking Bear to the camp but he stopped them.

"I will go alone." He said without looking back.

"Put down your guns!" Adam ordered. "If anyone accidently shoots Talking Bear we won't live to see tomorrow."

Two Stars walked out toward Talking Bear to show that she wasn't being hurt or held against her will. Talking Bear gave a smile when he saw Two Stars coming toward him safe and unharmed.

"I wonder what she is telling him." Adam wondered.

"What's going to happen now?" Ruth asked as she joined John and Adam. "I think she is trying to get him to let us go." John said as Ruth reached him. As Adam's eyes met John's he looked at his son as a man now. They all watched as Two Stars turned back toward the camp and began walking. Talking Bear headed back to where he had left Red Hawk and Gray Wolf waiting.

"What's he going to do?" Adam was asking even before Two Stars had reached them.

Two Stars said nothing until she stood in front of John. "Talking Bear wants all the whites to leave the mountain." Two Stars said then turned to Adam. "He has agreed to let John and his family stay. As for the rest, they must go." Two Stars told Adam as she looked at the rest of the people.

"Go where?" Adam asked.

"These people came here with me because of what I told them about the land."

"Talking Bear said if they will go to the river and make their camp and promise not to come back to the mountain, he will leave them alone."

"Be sure and tell them that if one of them comes back here they all will die." Two Stars told John that she had done all she could for his people and it was up to them from here on. As Two Stars looked away from John, she saw Red Hawk ride into view.

"Take your family to the land by the cabin and wait." Two Stars said as she walked toward where Red Hawk waited for her. "I'll see you tomorrow." She said without looking back at John.

Adam could feel every eye on him as he walked to the center of the camp. Questions seemed to come at Adam from all directions at one time.

"What are the Indians going to do?" One of Adam's younger brothers asked. "Are they coming back?" Another asked even before Adam could answer the first man.

After Adam got the group he said, "Yes and no." Then fell silent.

"Well which is it?" A man asked from the back of the bunch.

Talking Bear said, "That if you go back to the river and make your settlement, that he will leave you be." Adam fell quiet again before he went on, "My family will stay here with John."

"Did you make a deal with the Chief to get the land for yourself?" His brother asked.

Everyone saw the anger come to Adam's face.

"The only deal I made with the Chief was so you could live to see another sunrise little brother. If anyone thinks they can do a better job step up."

"It's hard to explain." Adam said. "As long as you stay by the river and don't come back to the mountain you will live. The only other option is to go back to Virginia on what little food you have. I can't make that decision for you." Adam said as the crowd fell quite. "As for me and my family, we are staying here." Adam told them in a tone that left no doubt that his mind was made up. Everyone seemed to drift back to their wagons in silence.

"John, you and James get things packed and ready to go while I go find us a good spot." Adam said.

"If you hurry George, we can have a new campsite by sundown." Adam said as he rode off.

"Yes Master Adam. Wes be ready to go as soon as you get back." George said to Adam's back as he rode away. "I'll have Liz and Emma start packing up the cooking supplies Master John." George told John as he walked off.

"James, it looks like we got the rest." John said.

Talking Bear sat by a blazing fire telling Red Hawk and Snow Beaver his planes for the white settlers. Only a few whites will stay here and the rest must go and live by the river he told them. That way if the Shawnee attack again they will hit the white settlers first. Two Stars came up just in time to hear the last of what Talking Bear was saying. Two stars couldn't understand why what Talking Bear was saying bothered her but it did. Two Stars made her way back to her teepee without letting herself be seen. She tried her best to put what she heard out of her mind but couldn't. Her thoughts were filled with the young boy she now called her husband. Somehow he was the key to filling the dream she has had since childhood; the dream of being the mother to the next Chief of the tribe; a Chief over seven villages and 1,000 braves. Two stars saw a catch in her dream. All Two Stars had to do is have a male child and if Talking Bear didn't her son becomes Chief. To make her dream come true she was going to need John, the boy, her husband. The only children that Talking Bear had now were the two girls. One Feather was the youngest and the closest to Two Stars. Morning Star was the oldest and a female copy of Talking Bear. She was always getting in trouble here lately; Two Stars had blamed it on her age. Morning Star had just turned fifteen and a few of the braves have been after her. Two Stars loved her but not like she did One Feather, the twelve year old. All this thinking was making Two Stars very sleepy so she walked to her bed and lied down.

"You know if I do this right I could be a mother by the time the snow comes?" Two Stars asked herself as she patted her belly.

Her dreams were filled with John's face.

"Master John, does you think them Indians will leave us alone now?" George asked.

"Yes George. I think they will." John told him as he helped George load a barrel of water.

John noticed Adam coming back as he pushed the water barrel into place. Ruth too had seen Adam coming and ran to where John and George stood.

"Adam Huff, I've been worried sick about you out there all alone." Ruth told him as soon as Adam got back to camp. "And it's not like I didn't have enough to worry about with John and that old Indian women."

John's thoughts of Two Stars were a lot of things, but old wasn't one of them. Adam didn't even take time to get off his horse before he was telling them let's go. Adam led them a mile past the cabin before he stopped them. The hill above the creek was fat and covered with dead trees.

"Isn't this beautiful?" Adam asked as he looked things over. As soon as James got the wagon stopped Ruth was climbing down off of it. Ruth stared at the place for a long time before she spoke. All Ruth could see was a lot of dead trees and knee high grass.

"We'll build two cabins to start with." Adam was saying as he climbed down from his horse. "I mean look at all these trees here in our own front yard." Adam said with a big smile.

When John looked at trees, he saw something different than Adam. He saw where something so strong coming through there had ripped the trees out of the ground.

"What kind of a wind could pull a 1,000 year old tree up; roots and all?" John started to say something to Adam about his question but as soon as he saw the smile on his father's face, he couldn't. Ruth didn't have any trouble speaking her mind.

"Adam what you think done them trees like that?" Ruth asked.

The next morning Two Stars decided to go to the cabin to give it a good cleaning. You know like she used to do for Dan Gains before he ran off. Two Starz's thoughts were on how she could get John into her bed. She knew that she fired his blood by the way he looked at her the first time they met. I'll put the bear skin on the bed so he will know that he is welcome there she thought. Thoughts of the bed and bear skin soon left Two Starz's mind once she stepped through the cabin door. A blood trail on the floor showed where the Shawnee brave had been drug out of the cabin. As Two Stars scanned the inside of the cabin she knew that it was going to take her all day. Two Stars wasn't sure if John was even coming back to the cabin or not. If he did she was going to put her dream into action she thought as she put the bear skin on the bed. As she reached down and picked up the bear skin Two Stars realized that John wouldn't even know what the skin meant to her. She had never told him that if the skin was on her bed he would be welcomed there. She had done this with Dan and he got to understand the meaning. A loud noise, from outside, brought Two Starz's eyes to the cabin door. Not knowing if it was John or a Shawnee brave that had gotten away Two Stars stood at the door with her knife drew back to kill. Maybe coming back here tonight wasn't such a good idea Two Stars told herself. As the sound got closer Two Stars could hear her heart pounding in her chest. The closer the sound got the more at ease Two Stars became. The sound of John's boots on the wood floor of the porch told her it was John.

"Shawnee braves don't wear boots." She told herself as she lowered the knife.

She laid the knife down as John entered.

A big smile came on John's face when he saw that Two Stars was there at the cabin waiting for him.

"It's me, John." He said as he remembered what happened to the brave that barged in.

Two Stars already knew who it was and sat at the table waiting for John to come in. John could tell that the knife had just been put down from the way it was still moving.

"I see you have been cleaning." John said as his blue eyes scanned the room.

The first thing John noticed was that the bear skin that was his bed now was spread on the bed. Two Stars watched as John's eyes went from the corner to the bed with the bear skin.

"I can move it back if you like." Two Stars said then waited quietly for John's reply.

John was confused by her words but he refused to let it show. "No that's alright." He said as he pulled out a chair and sat down across from Two Stars.

Two Stars saw as his eyes locked on the knife.

"You can never tell." She told him then moved it.

"Thank you for that." John said. "Sharp knives in the hands of a beautiful woman tend to make me nervous." He said with a smile. "Besides I have seen what happened to the last man who came in here uninvited." John said laughing.

"You are not a man yet." Two Stars told John and she wasn't laughing. The smile left John's face as he looked at her. Two Stars thought she may have gone too far with her comment so she changed the subject.

"Are you hungry?" She asked as she rose from the table.

Ruth had made John eat before he left the camp but he said yes anyway.

"You can take a bath while I cook." Two Stars said pointing to a bucket of water.

The whole time she was fixing the food Two Starz's eyes never left John. As he removed each piece of clothing John showed her a well formed body. His young body looked as if it had been carved out of stone. So different was he from Dan she thought.

Talking Bear had sent Gray Wolf around to each village and ordered the Chiefs to come for a meeting. After all the Chiefs were sitting around the camp fire Talking Bear rose to speak.

"You are my people and when I speak I speak for all the people." He said. I have given my word that the white by the river are not to be harmed. I have given them that place so they can warn us if the Shawnee should attack us again. I have spoken for the people and you will not break my word." Talking Bear told them.

"What about the one living with Two Stars?" Red Hawk asked.

"They are the words of my father and I can do nothing to change them." Talking Bear knew if he killed all the whites that an army of whites would come to the mountain for revenge. Dan Gains had told him that someday the whites would outnumber the trees. Talking Bear could now see how true he was.

The night air seemed cool to John's wet skin as he went about his bath. He could feel Two Starz's eyes watching his every move and it made him very uncomfortable. She was looking at him as if he was a piece of meat in the smokehouse. Two Stars looked at John's hard muscular body and marveled at how different it was from Dan's. He had to know that she was watching him but she just couldn't take her eyes off John. Two Stars was sure John knew when he turned his back to her and started dressing.

"Maybe I'm trying to go to fast." Two Stars thought as she watched John get dressed as fast as he could.

"It bothers you for me to look at you?" she asked as John sat down at the table.

"No. No." John said as he kept his eyes looking away from Two Stars. Two Stars smiled as she rose from the table and walked to the bed. John watched as Two Stars yanked the bear skin off the bed and threw it back onto the floor.

Adam sat on a pile of logs that was now ready to be shaped for the cabin. He was very proud of how much he, George, and the boys had gotten done in just two weeks. He saw that Two Stars was walking with

John this morning. It was the first time she had come there since the morning of the attack. Adam was a little worried that Ruth might say something to offend Two Stars. He hoped not.

"Go on." John said as him and Two Stars reached where Adam was sitting.

Both Adam and John watched as Two Stars headed toward where the women sat. The whole time she walked she was looking back over her shoulder at John. It didn't take long and Two Stars felt like one of the family. It seemed to Two Stars that every eye in the camp was on her. She knew now how John had felt the night she had watched him wash himself. Two Stars didn't like the feeling at all.

"Master Adam, that Indian girl done got Lizz and Emma wrapped around her finger." George said as he joined John and Adam. "Emma thinks she is a big sister I think." George went on to say.

"Two Stars makes them feel safe." Adam said as he turned his eyes toward the village.

"Pa, what do you think has happened to the ones that went to the river?" John asked.

"I don't know but as soon as I get the cabin built I'm going to see." Adam said as he turned back to John.

It was true that Talking Bear had left him and John alone but he wasn't sure if those by the river were doing as good.

"Where is James?" Adam asked when he noticed that James wasn't with them.

"Oh. Master James done went down to the creek to fetch some water." George said pointing toward the creek.

Adam turned to George and told him to get the tools and follow him as he headed to the trees. John smiled as he followed the two men.

Two Stars noticed how Emma watched her every move and it made her a bit uneasy. She knew that Emma didn't mean any harm in it but she still didn't like it. Emma couldn't get over how much Two Stars looked like a light skinned slave. If it wasn't for her deer skin dress she looked like Emma herself.

"What is the matter Emma?" Liz asked when she saw Emma staring at Two Stars.

"Oh nothing, I was just wondering how Miss Two Stars would look in one of my dresses."

"You mind your manners girl." Liz told her as she pointed a finger at Emma. "Miss Two Stars wouldn't want one of your old dresses!" Liz said loudly.

"I have more dresses at home." Two Stars said with a smile to show Emma she was forgiven.

Two Stars couldn't understand how the white people thought they could own land.

Now they say they have the right to own people as well. I would seek death before becoming a slave. Two Stars had made up her mind when Dan had left that she would never be owned by a man again.

Two Stars was glad that John was treating her like a wife instead of a slave. As Two Stars looked to where John was working with the other men she smiled. She watched as John put down the tool he was holding to wipe the sweat from his eyes. John was glad that Ruth was making Two Stars feel welcome. He had been worried that she would not accept Two Stars into the family. John remembered when he told Ruth that Two Stars was his wife, and she was going to have to accept her. John's thoughts drifted back to last night and the bear skin on the bed. He remembered how when he was taking his bath, Two Stars came to him and took the washcloth from him. A smile crossed John's face as he remembered how she stopped his protesting. John's thoughts went to where Two Stars took the washcloth from his hand and began to gently wash him. John was so deep in thought that he didn't see Emma coming to him carrying a bucket of water.

"Master John, what is you looking at?" Emma asked when she reached where John stood staring into space.

"Now girl you just leave Master John alone." George said as he called Emma to him.

"He got more important things to do than answer your foolish questions." George said with a wink and a smile to John.

Emma didn't understand a thing George was talking about, the only thing she saw was how it made Master John look sick.

"I hope you gets to feeling better Master John." Emma said as she headed back toward camp.

"Pay no mind to that silly girl." George said as the two watched Emma go.

George could have sworn that he saw John blush before he turned to leave. George smiled as he watched John walk away.

It was late evening by the time John and Two Stars reached their cabin.

"How long before the snow comes?" John asked as they walked through the cabin door.

"Six or seven months." Two Stars said as she led John through the door.

John stopped and turned to look how low the sun had sat already. It was so low that the trees had blended into a dark black shadow. John's thought of how cool the nights got and how when he was with Two Stars how hot, she made his blood run. When Two Stars looked John in the face, there was no doubt what was on his mind. Tonight Two Stars told herself, tonight she could know if it was her or Dan who was the reason she was childless. After tonight, she would know for sure if it was Dan's age that was the reason, not her.

John's lean body showed his young age, but the fire he started was built by a man. Two Stars leaned over and picked up the skin. Two Stars almost laughed out loud as she remembered the first-time John had made love. John was so nervous that he shook like a new-born wolf cub. She had to give him credit for one thing, he was a fast learner. The fear that John was going to yell at her like Dan had done was long gone. John had never raised his voice or his hand to her from that first day. What few times he had gotten mad at her, he just walked off and left her standing. Sometime Two Stars felt like she was hurt more that way than if John had slapped her. Two Stars remembered when she had told herself that she wouldn't fall in love with John. She soon learned that there was no defiance against kindness. Two Stars watched as the bear skin landed on the bed and a smile appeared on John's face. So he finally knows the meaning that the bear skin holds; Two Stars thought as she saw that John was already getting undressed.

Talking Bear and two braves sat in the woods where they could watch the cabin.

It had been almost a moon since Two Stars had come back to the village, and he come to see why.

"Somehow, I don't think the boy could stop Two Stars from coming to the village, if she wanted to come." Gray Wolf said.

"Maybe he has her chained like they do their slaves." Snow Beaver said, trying to anger Talking Bear into a fight.

The three watched as the cabin door opened and John walked out. "Good morning Talking Bear." John was saying as Two Stars stepped out behind John.

"You haven't been to the village in so long that I have come to see why." Talking Bear said when Two Stars came into view.

"I'm sorry brother, I've been so busy around here that I have just lost track of time." Two Stars said.

"You will come to the village today." Talking Bear ordered.

It was a voice of a Chief and not brother.

"You can go to the village if you want, I'll go help pa." John said as he stared at Talking Bear.

The eyes that stared back at him burned with anger. Talking Bear didn't need to say a word for John to understand that his sister didn't need his permission to go where she wanted.

"He wasn't giving his permission Talking Bear." Two Stars said in John's defense.

"I will come because I long to see my people, not because you ordered it." Two Stars snapped back at Talking Bear.

John, along with the two young braves, saw the fire in Two Starz's black eyes as she spoke. Now that was the sister, he remembered, Talking Bear thought to himself. John thought that Two Stars might have over stepped her place until he saw Talking Bear smile. She was more of a mother to Talking Bear than a sister seeing as she raised him from age five. Their mother had died during child birth, and the baby was born dead as well.

"Bring the boy if you want." He said as he left.

Talking Bear stopped just a few feet away and turned back to Two Stars.

"It's time he learned the way of our people and the laws of them as well." Talking Bear said.

Giving John another look over, he and the braves turned and left.

John was excited to finally get the chance to see the village and Two Stars people.

Two Stars couldn't explain the hint of fear she felt of going home. She wasn't sure of just how John was going to be accepted. She would find out today; she told herself as she got ready to leave.

"No." she said as she watched John reach for the gun in the corner.

"These are my people you will not need that; if someone harmed a person in the village while they are under its protection, the whole village would see them dead."

What Two Stars was saying made John feel safe but the look on Two Starz's face was what worried him the most right then.

Gray Wolf and Snow Beaver had been sent to find Red Hawk. Talking Bear had sent Red Hawk to see what the whites by the river were up to. Talking Bear knew that it was a long trip to the river but Red Hawk should be getting back by now he thought. As Talking Bear reached the creek the ears of his horse shot up like flags telling Talking Bear that there was something wrong.

Emma's eyes looked up the stream then down to make sure that there was no one around but her. She stood by a deep pool of water so clear Emma could see the bottom of the creek. Emma had grown tired of taking a bath in a wash basin. The fear that the water would be cold didn't out way the longing to take a bath. To take a bath means I am going to have to take off my dress; Emma thought as she checked the creek just once more. Being sure that she was alone, Emma took off her dress and laid it in the dry. After Emma had seen that the dress wasn't going to get wet, she let her eyes check the creek again. As she entered the cold water it almost took her breath away. Emma had been in the water a few seconds when she heard the horse behind her. Emma didn't know if it was fear or the cold water that made her skin craw with goose bumps. There behind Emma sat Read Hawk smiling at her as she tried to hide her nakedness.

Emma's thin arms just were not big enough to hide Emma's large breast.

"You don't have to fear me." Red Hawk said as Emma jumped to her feet and ran to where she had put her dress.

All fear left Emma when she saw Red Hawk kick his horse in the flanks and ride off. Emma stood watching as Red Hawk rode away unaware that she didn't put the dress on yet. Emma felt herself blush once she realized that she was still naked. As soon as Red Hawk vanished from sight Emma jerked up to the dress and put it on.

Adam pulled his pocket watch out and looked at it for the second time in ten minutes.

"It seven o'clock and John hasn't shown up yet." Adam told himself as he placed the watch back into his pocket.

Adam was becoming more worried by the minute.

"It wasn't like John to be this late, unless there was something wrong." Adam told himself as he looked toward the creek bed.

"He be alright Master Adam." George said as he too looked for a sign of John.

"Your right George, he has been working hard here in the day, and you can just imagine what Two Stars has him doing at night."

George could tell that Adam's laugh was a forced one.

George said nothing more as he watched Adam stare in the direction of Two Starz's cabin.

"I could go to the cabin and see why he did not show up." James said as he joined the two men.

"He not showed up yet?" Ruth was asking even before she reached the group of men.

James thought that he would help Adam sooth his mother's fears by repeating what he had learned.

"He's alright maw, he has just been putting too much work in at night isn't that right pa?" James blurted out.

Adam was speechless as he saw Ruth's mouth fly open and her green eyes searched out his.

"You should be ashamed of yourself Adam Huff, telling that boy such stories." Ruth said as she turned and left.

Adam felt his face blush as he watched her leave and turned to find both George and James staring at him.

"Let's get to work boys." Adam said loudly as he picked up the posthole diggers and walked off.

Both James and George found themselves staring at one another before selecting a tool and followed Adam. Gray Wolf sat in his hiding place, watching the whole thing unseen. Gray Wolf had been so close that he had heard every word the whites were saying.

John noticed how everyone stopped what they were doing to watch them as they rode into the village. John wasn't sure if it had been out of respect for Two Stars or in fear of him. Two Stars finely brought the horse to a stop in front a teepee with many drawings on it. A girl with long black hair came running out holding her arms out to her friend.

"Two Stars, you have come home." Little Dove said as she took Two Stars into her arms.

Little Dove was the sister to Red Hawk, Talking Bear's friend and number one brave. Both Two Stars and Little Dove were older sisters to boys.

"I was starting to think that you were never going to come back." Little Dove was saying as she gave Two Stars a big hug.

The whole time she was hugging Two Stars, she never took her eyes off John. "A bit younger than you thought he would be, isn't he?" Little Dove asked as she stepped back, away from Two Stars then laughed.

"It only takes a small spark to start a roaring fire." Two Stars said to get Little Dove to take her eyes off John.

"What?" Little Dove asked as she turned her eyes to Two Stars. "I can see that the fire still burns hot in this one." Little Dove said laughingly as she turned her eyes back to John.

"What should I do?" John asked as the two girls headed for Little Dove's teepee.

"You can just walk around the village and get to know the people."

Seeing how John looked so frightened Two Stars turned to him, "no one will harm you here you are under the protection of the whole village."

"No one would risk their life to harm you John." Two Stars said as she turned and went into the teepee with Little Dove.

John remembered when Two Stars had told him not to show fear because they saw it as a weakness. John turned and slowly walked toward his fate.

Emma couldn't forget how the Indian brave at the creek had looked at her that day.

It seemed to her when he spoke all her fear vanished with his words. His dark eyes didn't look at her naked body it looked through it. She remembered feeling them cling to her soul as he spoke.

It was as if his eyes had sat her soul free. Emma had never felt free before that day and now she longed to feel that way again.

"Is you sick girl?" Liz asked as she watched Emma staring out toward the creek.

"No maw, I was just thinking about going to get some water is all." Emma told Liz.

"I'll tell you what girl, as much as you like water you should have been a duck." Liz said with a laugh.

"You best stay away from that creek girl; you know what happened the last time." Liz said.

"The next time you might not get so lucky as you was before," Liz told Emma while pointing her finger at her.

Emma started to say something when she saw George coming toward her and knew it would be a waste of time. Ruth saw by the look on George's face that there was something wrong.

"What is it George?" Ruth asked even before George reached them.

"Master John never showed up today so Master Adam went looking for him Miss Ruth."

"I'm sure Master John be alright Miss Ruth, he just taking a day off." George said then lowered his eyes so Ruth couldn't see the doubt that showed in them.

"Master Adam say he was going to the cabin and see if the boy was there. He say for you not to worry, he will be back shortly." George said as his eyes went back to Ruth.

"I'm sure they both be alright Miss Ruth." Liz said as she took Ruth by the hand.

Adam stopped his horse at a trail turned toward the village and thought of going there to find out if John had gone there.

John soon lost his fear of the people in the village as he walked around watching them as they went about their task. He found that just about everyone looked at him as if he were a stray dog that had wondered into the village lost. Most of them would look him over once then go back to what they were doing. Gray Wolf was just entering Talking Bear's teepee, as John reached it. John stopped just outside the teepee before making up his mind to go in. Once his eyes had gotten use to the dim light in the teepee John could see the four sitting in a circle. There sat Talking Bear, Red Hawk, and two braves that John didn't know. When the man with his back to him turned around John saw that it was the trapper Gains. John couldn't explain it but seeing Gains there he felt a lot more at ease.

"Come and sit with us." Talking Bear said pointing to a place beside the trapper.

"You know that if my brother hadn't taken the pelt with him when he left I would have been the one living with Two Stars, now don't you?" Gaines asked as John sat down.

John's eyes were on Talking Bear as Gains was talking and he could swear that a smile crossed Talking Bear's face. John thought it meant that Talking Bear was glad it hadn't gone that way as he watched the smile disappear.

"You treating my sister well?" Talking Bear asked as he turned his eyes to John.

The question seemed to surprise every one there except Red Hawk. The question surprised Gains as much as it did John so he turned his eyes to John and waited in silence for John's answer.

John's eyes scanned the room and found that every eye there was staring at him.

"Yes, I treat her well and she has been a good wife since the first time we met." John said as he turned his eyes toward Gains.

As John turned his eyes back he saw it. There in Talking Bear's hand was the beaver pelt.

"Gains was just saying as to how your people didn't know the meaning of this pelt; it rightly belonged to him. He said you didn't know that it was a gift from the people for the life of a Chief. My sister is a gift from our people and by our laws we cannot tell Dan Gains what he can do with a gift. When you were sold the pelt its meaning stayed the same." Talking Bear said then turned his gaze to Gains.

John started to say something when Talking Bear put up a hand to stop him. "You go." Talking Bear said to Gains when he saw that Gains wanted to hear what John had to say.

"I will tell you now that I don't like the idea of my sister's blood mixing with yours. As a Chief I must go by the law of the people and I will but as Two Starz's brother I'll not let you turn her into a red slave." Talking Bear said loudly.

John waited until he was sure Gains was gone before he spoke. "Talking Bear, I'm in love with Two Stars and I think she loves me. I'm not trying to turn Two Stars into anything like a slave of any color." John said just as loud.

"Your sister can go as she pleases and I couldn't stop her if I wanted." John told Talking Bear to the surprise of the other braves in the teepee.

The little pep talk Two Stars had given about not showing fear must have worked for John. John saw that Talking Bear's face was wearing a big smile. It was at this time that Talking Bear started looking at John as a man instead a boy.

"Your spirit is strong." Talking Bear said with a hint of fear in the words.

"What about my family, are they in any danger?" John asked. "As long as my sister is married to you they are safe. If they break a village law, you all will die."

Two Stars was really enjoying spending the day with her best friend, Little Dove.

She had missed talking to someone that she could tell anything too. When they last talked, Two Stars had told Little Dove that no matter what she wasn't going to fall in love with that boy. If he tried to abuse her she would kill him herself. Two Stars had prepared herself for everything but the boy's kindness. She soon learned that she hadn't prepared herself for everything like John's lust for her. Two Stars was surprised to find that John's passion for her only drove her passion higher.

Little Dove's question about John brought Two Stars back to her friend.

"Tell me, what's a young white stud like in bed?" Little Dove asked pointing outside.

Two Starz's eyes looked around the teepee to make sure they were the only ones there before she answered her friend.

"He is as different from Dan as night and day." Two Stars said with a blush.

"Did he know what to do or did you have to teach him?" Little Dove asked in a high pitched voice.

Two Stars knew that John wouldn't like her talking about their sex life but she had to tell somebody.

"John was a virgin that first night but he caught on fast." Two Stars found herself saying.

Little Dove's face lite up as she brought her hand up to her open mouth.

"Have you got a baby in there yet?" Little Dove asked as she put her hand on Two Starz's belly.

"I'm not sure but I was supposed to have started last week," Two Stars said as she placed her hand over Little Dove's.

"It's still too early to tell." Two Stars said as she lifted her hand off Little Dove's.

"You know if you have a male child it could become tribal Chief someday." Little Dove said as she took back her hand.

"Talking Bear has children," Two Stars said.

John noticed how Two Stars wasn't saying much on the way back to the cabin. He thought of asking her if something was wrong but decided against it. She will tell me sooner or later he told himself. Two Stars was thinking about what Little Dove had said about Talking Bear not having a son. According to the village law, if she had a male child and Talking Bear didn't before he died her and John's boy would become Chief. It didn't matter anyway, Talking Bear was still young enough he could have a lot of son's before he died she thought.

Two Stars turned her eyes toward the setting sun and said in a low voice, "I don't care if it's a boy or a girl, just give me a child I can call my own." She was saying as the cabin came into sight.

As John entered the cabin he felt the heat coming off the roaring fire that Two Stars had built.

Two Starz's actions were starting to worry John.

"Is something wrong?" John asked in worried voice.

"No, no, there is nothing wrong." Two Stars said as she turned her back to John.

"I guess I'm just tired from the long day is all." Two Stars told John as she stared into the fire.

"If there was you would tell me, wouldn't you?" John asked as he turned Two Stars to face him.

Two Stars let her arms drop to her side as she stepped back from John. She did this so she could get a better look at his face and see his reaction when he heard her words.

"Talking Bear is the tribal Chief now and if he has a son then the boy would be next in line. If my brother doesn't have a son before he dies and we did then our son would become the next Chief."

John got a strange look on his face.

"Are you saying you are going to have a baby?" John asked as if he was in shock.

"No, no, John I'm not saying that; I'm just saying someday maybe it could happen." Two Stars said.

"Good." John said.

She turned quickly to hide the tears in her eyes. John came up behind Two Stars and put his arms around her waist and kissed her on the back of the neck.

"We are too young to start a family." John said as he kissed her again.

Johns words stabbed at Two Starzs heart like a sharp knife.

When Two Stars turned to face John the tears in her eyes had been replaced by anger.

"Have it your way." Two Stars said as she pushed John to the side and walked to the bed.

John watched as she jerked the bear skin off the bed and threw it to the floor. It didn't stop until it had reached the corner where John had slept his rst night there.

"If you don't want kids there is no use in you sleeping in my bed!" Two Stars yelled.

"I didn't say I didn't want kids, all I said was now is not the time!" John yelled back.

Even though Two Stars had felt John's anger, her anger was even greater.

"I know what you said." Two Stars told John as she tossed his pillow on top of the bear skin.

John was lying on the hard wood floor trying to understand what he had said to make Two Stars so angry. Was he wrong for wanting to wait to start a family? The more John thought about it the more he was convinced he had made the right decision.

"Maybe John is right." Two Stars told herself as she stared at the darkened ceiling.

Maybe it was too soon to think about a child but a woman only has so much time to have kids and Two Stars could feel her time slipping by.

"It's all in the hands of the Great Spirit anyway." Two Stars told herself as she stared into the darkness.

Two Stars took the back of her hand and wiped tears from her swollen eyes and drifted off to sleep.

It was just getting light when John woke up the next morning. Once he was able to get his eyes focused he looked at Two Stars still asleep on the bed. John quietly made his way outside and left. Adam stood staring at the path that led to John's and Two Starz's cabin. George rose from his seat on the pile of logs right beside the half built cabin. Adam didn't even notice George as he walked up behind him.

"Master Adam the boy will be here today I'm sure." George said as he stopped behind Adam.

"I know your right George." Adam said without taking his eyes off the path.

The sound of a horse coming toward them drew both Adam's and George's eyes toward the sounds direction. John saw that Adam and George stood watching as he rode up.

"You see Master Adam I told you that Master John would be here." George said loudly.

Adam waited for John to get off his horse before saying anything to him. "What happened to you yesterday?" Adam asked as soon as John got off his horse.

"Two Stars took me to her village to meet her people." John said.

Adam gave a sigh of relief then hugged John.

"Well you're here now and that's what counts." Adam was saying as he guided John to where the women were making something to eat.

No one was happier to see John that morning than James. The whole day Adam had yelled at him over the slightest mistake. James knew that Adam had been worried about John so he took it like a man. James had been thinking of John too but James thought as long as John was with Two Stars they were safe. After everyone had eaten Emma came to ask James if he would go with her to fetch water.

"Emma you got nothing to be afraid of." James said.

"Go ahead Emma, its safe enough." John told her.

As Emma turned her eyes back to James she saw him pointing his finger toward the creek.

"Now you go do what Master John done told you girl." George said as he rose from his seat.

Emma picked up the water buckets and left.

Talking Bear had ordered Red Hawk to go watch the white camp and report what they were doing. Red Hawk had watched John ride into camp almost an hour ago but nothing since.

Red Hawk thought of how different his people treated their captives than the whites did their black slaves. As he sat thinking he saw that these whites treated their slaves like part of the family. It was completely different from what Dan Gains had told them.

"I would die before I became a slave." Red Hawk told himself as his eyes went to the camp again.

The buckets swung back and forth as Emma packed them down the path toward the creek. Emma stopped at the creek bank and looked both up and down it making sure there was no one else there. Once she was sure she was the only one there she got down on her knees to dip the water. The ripples the bucket made on the water acted like a mirror to the morning sun. Emma watched it until it reached the other side.

Red Hawk stepped out from behind a bush just as the ripple reached the other shore.

Red Hawk's reflection on the water was the first hint that Emma got that she wasn't alone.

She shot to her feet then walked backward toward the creek. She had kept the water pail in her hand as she rose. Emma could feel the cold water as it ran quickly over her feet before she stopped.

"Don't be afraid I will not hurt you." Red Hawk said as he walked toward Emma.

Emma didn't know why but she wasn't afraid of this Indian, maybe it was his English he spoke.

"I'z not afraid, Master Indian." Emma said as she lowered the bucket. Even after Emma had said that she wasn't afraid of Red Hawk she felt goose bumps when he stood right in front of her. Emma flinched as Red Hawk took his finger and brought it down the side of Emma's face. The girl's skin is just a little lighter than mine, Red Hawk thought as his hand fell to his side. Red Hawk could tell from Emma's eye's that he was being studied. Red Hawk stood in silence and let Emma's eyes get their fill of him. No hair on his face and chest like the white people and her pa, Emma thought as she studied Red Hawk. His long black hair hung in braids down both sides of his head.

"His eyes were almost as black as his hair." Emma told herself as her green one's looked at his.

Red Hawk knew that he shouldn't have let himself be seen but his curiosity about the slave girl had gotten the best of him.

Their silence was broken by James as he came down the path calling Emma's name.

Emma had turned toward the sound of James's voice just for a second. When she turned back to Red Hawk, he was gone not leaving any sign that he was ever there. Emma stood staring at the woods when James reached her.

"What's the matter?" James asked her as he stopped.

"I thought I heard something Master James." Emma said as she stared into the woods.

"It was just some animal getting itself a morning drink." James told Emma as he began to stare at the trees also.

Seeing nothing James turned to face Emma.

"You get them buckets filled and get yourself back to camp." James ordered.

"Yes Master James, I'll do that right now." Emma was saying as she reached for the buckets.

By the time Emma had retrieved the buckets James had turned and headed back up the path that led to the wagons. Emma dipped the two buckets of water then looked where Red Hawk had vanished. There was no sign of the Indian but Emma kept looking over her shoulder as she walked.

Two Starz's heart pounded like a drum as she woke up to find John already gone. Fear was replaced by a smile on Two Starz's face as her eyes saw that John hadn't taking his things with him when he left. She still had a chance to become a mother.

Talking Bear sat on the ground in front the campfire he kept in his teepee. He hailed a pipe in one hand while the other one picked a small branch from the fire. Talking Bear's eyes stayed on Red Hawk even as he put the stick to the pipe and puffed.

"I saw the boy that wed Two Stars enter the camp and she was not with him." Red Hawk said as he kept his eyes on the ground.

Talking Bear never knew Red Hawk to give him a report without looking him in the eyes.

"Is there something else?" Talking Bear asked as he took another puff on the pipe.

Red Hawk brought his eyes up to meet Talking Bear's as he spoke. "I let myself be seen by the slave girl, I had to see if she was different." Red Hawk said.

"These whites have only been here for one moon and they are destroying the people of the village." Talking Bear's voice showed his anger.

"You will not let this happen again, do you understand?" Talking Bear yelled as he jumped to his feet.

Adam had noticed that John's mind wasn't here with his body, so he called John to him. By the time John had reached Adam he had sat down in the shade of a big oak tree.

"What's on your mind son?" Adam asked as soon as John took a seat.

John just looked at Adam in silence for a minute before he spoke.

"I had a fight with Two Stars pa." That's all John was saying as his eyes looked to make sure they were alone.

A smile crossed Adam's face as he placed his hand on John's shoulder.

"A fight is good for a marriage as long as the only thing getting thrown is words," Adam said.

"Two Stars wants to have a baby right away and I don't." John said looking at Adam's reaction.

"Hell son, you know how to fix that don't you?" Adam asked with a laugh.

"Don't sleep with her and she will not have a single one." Adam said with a louder laugh this time.

Adam saw that John didn't see the humor in his words and stopped laughing.

Two Stars started to clean the cabin and got most of it done before reaching the bear skin lying in the corner. Two Stars knew if she was to become a mother she would need to get John back into her bed. I will go tell him that I'm sorry about last night and welcome him back to my bed. Two Stars didn't even close the door behind her as she raced toward the path that would take her to John.

It had been Sam Masterson, who had come up with the idea that all he and Clay Huff, Adam's youngest brother, would need to do was steal the beaver pelt from John and Two Stars. Sam had told Clay that Two Stars would have to be their slave if they could get the pelt. Both Sam and Clay had left the camp by the river when the sickness broke out.

Clay had wanted to get his wife and daughter out of that camp before he left but Sam said, "No."

"Wait until we get the pelt before you say anything." Sam had told him. "Once we have the pelt, you can bring your wife Mary and your daughter Rose here to live with me and Two Stars." Sam had explained as they walked toward John's cabin.

"You see when I get control of Two Stars we will have control of the Indians and the whites."

Clay hadn't understood a single word Sam was saying but he did understand that his days of living at that river would be over. To have stayed there meant death for sure.

Adam and John had just placed the center beam in the cabin when John yelled, "Rider coming."

By the time Adam had gotten to the ground, John was already standing with Gains.

"Who are they?" John asked as Adam made his way toward them.

"I don't know." Gains was saying as Adam reached them.

Adam could tell from the look on Gains's face that this wasn't a pleasant morning call.

"What's going on?" Adam asked as he stopped.

Gains waited until they had rode off.

Two men from the camp by the river left, and Talking Bear had ordered their death.

"Maybe they just came for a visit." Adam said trying to get Gains to calm down.

"You don't understand Huff those two men attacked a young Indian girl in a nearby village."

"If they are tracked here by the Indians, you will all die. Do you understand?!" Gains yelled.

"The only reason you people are not dead is because of Two Stars."

"Talking Bear has protected you up until now but he would kill you himself before starting a tribal war."

"We had nothing to do with that!" John yelled as Gains got back on his horse.

Adam's face turned white when he realized just how dangerous things had changed.

"If I were you Mr. Huff, when those men do show up I would turn them over to Talking Bear."

"I couldn't do that these men we are talking about are my kin." Adam was saying as Gains rode off.

"It's your neck." Gains said without looking back.

While Adam explained what was going on to George and James, who had just reached him, John walked over and picked up his gun.

"Where are you going?" Adam asked when he saw John heading for his horse.

"I'm going to the cabin to tell Two Stars what is going on." John said as he mounted the horse.

"Ok." Adam said as he watched John ride off.

Red Hawk sat at Talking Bear's right as he talked to the Chiefs from the surrounding villages. This was a great honor to Red Hawk for him to be able to do this. This position showed that Red Hawk was Talking Bear's number one warrior. As Talking Bear spoke Red Hawk saw that the other Chiefs were calling for war against whites.

"You have protected these whites for too long now!" Blue Buck, the Chief of the village where the child was attacked, yelled.

"I don't like the whites either, but I am bound by my father's words to protect them!" Talking Bear yelled back.

"You can have the two from the river but the whites here are not to be harmed; is that clear Blue Buck?" Talking Bear said more quietly this time.

Blue Buck didn't like it but to go to war with Talking Bear meant going to war with the other villages under Talking Bear's control.

"You have my word." Talking Bear said to the remaining Chiefs as he got to his feet.

Red Hawk started to follow the Chiefs out until Talking Bear stopped him.

"Stay here, I need you to go to Two Starz's cabin and stay with her until this is over with." Talking Bear said after the others left.

"I will not fail you Talking Bear." Red Hawk said over his shoulder as he left. As Talking Bear watched Red Hawk leave he remembered a story Iron Bear "I will not fail you Talking Bear." Red Hawk said over his shoulder as he left. As Talking Bear watched Red Hawk leave he remembered a story Iron Bear told. It was the story of how a tribal war was fought back when Iron Bear first become tribal Chief. Talking Bear wasn't going to let the whites start a tribal war even if he had to kill all the whites himself.

Red Hawk wondered what was going to happen to the slave girl if war broke out. What was Two Stars going to say when he told her what he was there for?As Talking Bear's number one brave he couldn't question the Chief's orders.

"Why don't we go to the boy's cabin and steal the pelt?" Clay Huff asked as he and Sam Masterson hid in the bushes by the path.

"Clay, I think you are the dumbest man I have ever met!" Sam yelled as he turned to Clay.

"That boy isn't going to just hand over the pelt for nothing."

"What do we got that he will want?" Clay asked looking at their meager possessions.

"By the time John comes home we my friend will have the squaw." Sam said laughingly. "Gains told me that the cabin was down this creek somewhere." Sam went on to say as he turned his eyes toward the path again. "Once the boy hands the pelt over, we kill him and the squaw then say the Indians did it." "We just tell the Chief that the boy sold it to us before he was killed." Sam said without looking at Clay.

It was true that Clay didn't have any love for Adam's boys but the idea of killing one of them didn't set right with him. Clay knew he was in too deep now to turn back.

Two Starz's mind was on John and not on the danger that lay just up the path ahead. Two Stars first saw the two men when Sam Masterson stood up from behind a bush in front of her. Two Stars turned and ran toward the cabin and her knife she had left there. Two Stars was sure that the man had seen her so all she could do was out run him.

Clay watched as Two Stars ran back down the path she had just come from. Sam Masterson was so heavy set that it took him longer to get to his feet beside Clay.

"Don't just stand there boy get after her." Sam was saying as he got to his feet.

Clay started running after Two Stars and found that he was no match for her speed. As Clay stopped to catch his breath the cabin came in to view. Sam reached where Clay was standing just in time to see Two Stars go through the door. It took both Sam and Clay a while to get their breath back enough to talk.

"You don't have to be afraid of us missy, I am John's kin." Clay was saying as Two Stars slammed the door.

"We mean you no harm." Sam said with a little laugh.

"Do you think she's got a gun in there?" Clay asked when he got no reply.

"Well if she does, she has only got one shot." Sam was saying as he got behind Clay and pushed him forward.

"I don't know about this Sam." Clay said as he froze in his tracks.

"She might of went out the back and has gone for more Indians."

Sam hated to admit it but Clay just could be right about that.

"I'll tell you what Clay we'll sneak up on her and cover both doors just in case you're right." Sam said.

This isn't going to be as easy as Sam said it was going to be Clay thought as he followed Sam toward the cabin. With each step their hearts pounded louder. John noticed how a lot of small branches had been broken on the path back to the cabin. It appeared to John that some kind of large beast had been running toward the cabin. John kicked his horse in the flanks and put the animal in a dead run toward the cabin and Two Stars. Two Stars had found the knife and stood with it behind the doorway.

"I don't think she is going to give us the pelt." Clay said as the two reached the porch.

"Shut up you fool she can hear every word you say!" Sam yelled at Clay. The two men started yelling so loud that they didn't hear Red Hawk ride up behind them.

Red Hawk stopped his horse and came up behind them on foot. These must be the two that everyone is looking for Red Hawk told himself as he placed an arrow into the bow. As soon as Sam saw Red Hawk put an arrow in his bow he knew there would be no talking. Sam raised his gun just as Red Hawk shot at him. Red Hawk reached for another arrow just as soon as the first one left the string. The young man stepped in front of the arrow that had been shot at Sam and took the arrow instead. Red Hawk worked as fast as he could to get the second arrow into the bow. Sam had the gun pointed at him and was just about to fire when Red Hawk heard the sound of a gun going off behind him. John's shot had caught Sam in the head and he dropped like a rock. Red Hawk was surprised that he felt nothing then watched as Sam dropped to the ground. It wasn't until then that Red Hawk saw John standing behind him holding a smoking gun.

Two Stars slowly opened the door and stepped out on to the porch. Two Stars wasn't sure if what she had just seen was for real. To see a white man shoot another white man to save an Indian was unreal. John kept his eyes on Red Hawk as he lowered the gun not sure what he would do next. Red Hawk looked at John then turned and walked over and picked up the gun that Sam had dropped just before he died. John got off the horse and walked over to where Red Hawk was looking the gun over.

"You'll need these." John said as he bent over and picked up the bullets and powder horn from the dead man.

John wasn't sure but he thought he saw a smile on Red Hawk's face as he handed him the bullets.

"That sounded like it came from Master John's place." George said with fear in his voice.

"That second shot was John's but the other one wasn't." Adam said as he headed for his horse.

George went and got the guns while Adam saddled the horse. Ruth ran out to where Adam was and began asking him questions.

"Do you think that sound came from John's place?" She asked.

"Yes, I do." Adam told her as he tightened the saddle on the horse.

"I've shot that gun so many times that I would know the sound of it anywhere."

"Adam don't take James with you." Ruth said as she watched James run toward them.

"James you stay here with your maw and the girls." Adam said just as James reached him.

"But pa, John might be in trouble." James said as he handed Adam the gun he was caring.

"It could be that John was just shooting him something to eat!" Adam told them as he climbed into the saddle and road off. Adam said that to calm Ruth's fears as well as his own.

"But Pa." James was saying as he watched Adam ride off with George following behind him.

"Now James, your pa knows best." Ruth said as she led James back into the camp.

George had to run to try to keep up with Adam's horse. Adam was ahead of him but George never lost sight of Adam. Adam knew that the sound of the other gun had to be from the two men the Indians were after.

Up until that moment Red Hawk hadn't trusted any white man. When John handed Red Hawk his hand to shake Red Hawk was tempted to take it. Both men turned their heads and looked at the two dead men on the ground. Red Hawk seemed to be more interested in his new gun than the two dead white men at his feet. John, on the other hand, was kneeling down beside the body of his dead uncle. John had never had any love for Uncle Clay but he never wished him dead either. As for the other man John felt nothing even as John stared into his open eyes.

Adam reached the cabin just as Red Hawk was raising the gun into the air. As Adam started to take aim at Red Hawk, he saw the bodies of the two men on the ground.

"What's going on here John?" Adam asked as he lowered the gun and stopped his horse.

"It's the two from the river pa." John was saying just as George reached them.

"Pa one of them is Uncle Clay, they tried to break into the cabin and when Red Hawk tried to stop them they were going to kill us." John said to Adam.

Adam didn't seem to hear a word John was saying as he too knelt beside his younger brother's body.

"Thanks to Red Hawk, Two Stars is safe." John said as he stared at Adam.

John could feel Red Hawk flinch as he rose to his feet and placed a hand on his shoulder. Two Stars reached where the four men stood, talking, just as John did.

John noticed how George never took his eyes off Red Hawk taking in every move he made. This was the first time George had been this close to any Indian. George's eyes kept jumping from Red Hawk to John as Red walked up and stood right in front of George.

"Master John, what's he doing?" George asked as Red Hawk reached out a hand and placed it to George's face.

"Has he gone out of his head Master John?"

"No George, he just has never seen a black man before." John said with a laugh as Red Hawk rubbed his hand over George's face.

As soon as Red Hawk took down his hand from George he turned back to the two men lying at his feet.

"We must take these men back to the village and Talking Bear." Red Hawk said.

The words had no sooner left Red Hawk's mouth when Talking Bear came into view.

The Chief from the village beside the river rode beside him along with thirty braves.

"These are the two you're looking for Talking Bear," Red Hawk said pointing at the two on the ground.

Without a word Blue Elk rode up to where the two men lying face up staring at him.

Blue Elk turned to face Talking Bear and asked, "What of these?" Pointing at Adam and John.

"These are my people." Two Stars said as she stepped in front of John.

"My sister's words are my words." Talking Bear told Blue Elk.

"Talking Bear, you are tribal Chief and that is the only reason I don't rid our land of this white plague now."

Blue Elk spit at the two men on the ground then turned his horse leading his braves away.

Talking Bear turned his attention back to Adam and John. What

Blue Elk had said about this white plague Talking Bear felt the same way, only his father's word kept him from taking Blue Elk's side.

"Talking Bear, this boy saved my life." Red Hawk said as he pointed the gun he was holding at John.

"They saved my life as well brother." Two Stars said as she walked up to him. "This gun I took off of that one." Red Hawk said pointing at Sam. Everyone saw how Talking Bear's eyes were locked onto the gun Red Hawk.

"Red Hawk get Two Stars and your horse ready while she go's and gets her things." He ordered.

Two Stars wanted to show her brother that John was now one of the people. It also told Talking Bear that once she and John had a son he could someday become Chief.

"I'm not going anywhere brother." Two Stars said as she walked over and took John's hand.

"I will stay with my husband and his people and come to the village tomorrow."

Red Hawk saw the anger that flashed in Talking Bear's eyes. It even surprised Talking Bear that Two Stars would insult him in front of his braves.

"You will do as I say!" Talking Bear shouted in an angry loud voice. "This is not your village here Talking Bear." Two Stars said as she made a gesture at the woods with her hand.

"You are part of the people but the whites must go and leave this land forever." Talking Bear said as he turned his horse and left.

Red Hawk looked over his shoulder as he followed Talking Bear back toward the village.

They all stood in silence as he rode away.

"Is Talking Bear going to drive us away from here?" John asked with alarm in his voice.

"I have no idea what he is going to do." Two Stars said as she watched them vanish from sight.

"I think he is just mad because I went against his word in front of his braves." Two Stars said hoping she was right.

"John if you will help us we'll dig two graves." Adam said as he pointed for George to get ahold of Clay's feet.

John's eye's turned toward George and his pa before they returned to Two Stars. John just stared at her in silence before he spoke.

"Two Stars, I love you but if Talking Bear attacks my pa I will fight right beside him. To the death if need be." John said.

"Talking Bear was just mad at me is all." Two Stars said as she put both arms around John then laid her head on his chest.

"Besides, Talking Bear needs your people by the river to badly to attack them."

A puzzled look came to John's face.

"What do you mean 'needs' them?" John asked as he stepped back from Two Stars.

Two Stars got her own puzzled look as she asked, "Have I said too much already."

"He needs them." Two Stars told John as she pointed at the gun he was holding.

As soon as George and Adam had buried the two dead men they headed for home.

John was surprised to find Two Stars pouring his bath water when he came through the door. As John stood watching, Two Stars walked over to where the bear skin laid in the corner and picked it up. A smile crossed his lips as he watched her spread it across the bed. John had caught on to just what that gesture meant to her. John didn't know if it was because of his youth or what but he soon forgot everything that happened that day. Two Stars never took her eyes off John as she took off her dress and stood naked by the bed. John washed quickly then hurried to bed.

The sun had been up for an hour as Emma hurried and got the water buckets.

"Where are you going girl?" George asked as she headed for the door. "I'z going after water pa, so maw can make fresh coffee." Emma said as she held out the buckets.

"No you don't girl, you don't leave this camp unless Master James is with you." George said.

"What's the matter George?" Liz asked as she came up behind him. "I don't want her going to the creek without someone with her." George said.

"I thought you said that them Indians would leave us alone now that they caught them two men?" Liz asked as she stared at George.

"I know what I said women but I still don't trust them Indians." George said in a lower voice.

"Then you go with her." Liz said as she took one of the buckets from Emma's hand and handed to George.

John came down the path by the creek just about the same time George and Emma reached it. He was glad to see that Emma wasn't alone.

"Morning Master John." George said as John stopped his horse right in front of him.

"Morning Master John." Emma said as she put her arm over her eyes to block out the sun.

Never taking his eyes off the tree line John said, "Don't stay here too long," as he kicked the horse in the flanks and rode on into camp.

Emma watched as George got down on one knee to dip his water.

"The water is much better out here." Emma told George as she waited out into the stream.

Just as Emma put her bucket into the water she could tell the current was very strong. The current jerked the bucket from her hand and went drifting down stream.

"Go'z get that bucket and gets your water." George ordered as he stood at the bank.

"Ok pa, I'll get it." Emma said as she headed to where it had caught on some bushes.

Emma made her way very slowly to it. Just as Emma reached for the bucket a hand came from behind her and covered her mouth.

Emma's heart was pounding so fast she thought it was going to stop. Emma could hear George's voice yelling for her to hurry up but she was afraid to speak.

"I mean you no harm." The voice said in plain English from behind her.

"Will you not yell if I take my hand away?" The voice asked.

Without a sound Emma shook her head yes.

"I mean you no harm." Red Hawk said as he took his hand from Emma's mouth.

As Emma turned she was staring right into Red Hawk's black eyes. "You come with me and you will be free." Red Hawk told her once she was facing him.

Emma was surprised that an Indian could speak English as well as Red Hawk did.

"I'z as free as it gets for my people." Emma said after her heart got back to normal.

Emma spoke in a low voice as though she was afraid that George would hear her. Emma lost her fear enough that she reached out her hand toward the black braided hair that hung at the side of Red Hawk's head.

"I must go now." Emma said as she heard George calling for her again. "You choose to be a slave instead of free?" Red Hawk asked in a confused voice.

"No, I choose to stay with the people I love instead of being free in the woods." Emma told Red Hawk as she turned her eyes toward the sound of George's voice calling.

When Emma looked back she saw that Red Hawk had vanished just as quickly as he had appeared.

"Oh, there you are girl." George said when he saw Emma standing and staring at the woods.

"Girl you get that bucket filled so we can get out of here." George said angrily.

Emma was so deep in thought that she wasn't hearing a thing

George was saying.

"What good would being free do for me out in the middle of nowhere?" Emma asked herself.

"I'll be right there pa." she told him then left.

Red Hawk's thoughts were on the girl at the creek and the way she had turned his offer of freedom down.

He asked himself, "Should I tell Talking Bear about it or not?"

By the time Red Hawk reached the village he still hadn't made up his mind. As he entered the Teepee of the elder's Red Hawk found Talking Bear sitting in a circle of braves.

"Are you going to attack the whites at the river?" Snow Beaver asked loudly.

"We will wait and see what the braves that I sent there have to say!" Talking Bear yelled angrily.

"What about the whites by the creek?" Talking Bear asked Red Hawk when he saw him come in.

"The whites are acting just the same Talking Bear; they are staying close to their camp." Red Hawk decided to make his report as short as possible then sat in silence.

Snow Beaver started to say something until a look from Talking Bear told him that he too should stay silent as well.

"Two Stars said to tell you that she still love you as a brother but her decision to stay with the boy does not change." Red Hawk told him.

"My sister chose the boy over her people, she is no better than the whites to me!" Talking Bear yelled at Red Hawk.

"Talking Bear, we need to wipe these people off the lands handed down through our fathers." Snow Beaver cried as he jumped to his feet.

Red Hawk rose to his feet as well.

"We need the whites and their guns to guard the river against the crow raiding parties.

"You know that to attack them means a lot of our braves will die." Red Hawk said loudly.

Talking Bear knew what Red Hawk was saying made more since. If the crow did come back in force he would need the whites alive for now.

"Snow Beaver, you are to leave the whites alone for now. I'll have Red Hawk keep an eye on them." Talking Bear said as Snow Beaver sat back down.

Once Talking Bear said those words it was law.

As Talking Bear turned back to Red Hawk he said, "I want you to stop by Two Stars in the morning and tell her that she can come to the village."

"That will be good for the people," Red Hawk said with a big smile. "I'll take my sister, Little Dove, with me and she can stay with Two Stars while I watch the whites."

Talking Bear found Red Hawk's eagerness to go watch the whites kind of strange but soon put it out of his thoughts.

"I'm sure that Two Stars would like that." Talking Bear said as he watched Red Hawk leave.

"We'll talk more in the morning." Talking Bear said as he dismissed the rest of the braves.

Talking Bear waited until the last brave had left before he sat back down by the fire. If it wasn't for needing the whites by the river he would kill every one of them. If it wasn't for that beaver pelt and his father's word he would kill the boy too. Talking Bear was bound by the word of a tribal Chief; to break it it would mean his death.

The next morning Little Dove was surprised to see her brother walking toward her teepee.

Once Red Hawk met her at the door he told her she was to go with him and stay with Two Stars until he came back. Little Dove was glad to hear that she was going to get to see her best friend after what had happened between her and Talking Bear. She and Two Stars had grown up together as best friends raising their little brothers. They had done their best just keeping the two boys out of trouble. Both Red Hawk and Talking Bear made that a full time job. After Two Stars was given to Dan Gains she only got to see her a few times a year. Little Dove was starting to think that it was going to be the same with the boy Two Stars had married.

"Are you ready yet?!" Red Hawk yelled from outside.

Little Dove grabbed her things then hurried out to where Red Hawk was waiting for her.

"I would like to get there before dark," Red Hawk was saying as Little Dove mounted the horse.

"Don't be in such a hurry or I'll put you over my knee," Little Dove said with a laugh.

Two Stars opened her eyes and found that John had already gone. Her thoughts went to the love making her and John had made last night. She placed a hand on her bare belly and gently patted it. She was sure that John had given her a baby.

"You will grow up to be the Greatest Chief we have ever had." Two Stars said as she smiled.

The sound of horses outside made Two Stars grab her dress and run and lock the door. Two Stars slowly walked to where she could see out the window. Once she saw that it was Red Hawk and Little Dove she ran out to meet them.

"I must go now," Red Hawk said as he saw Two Stars come out of the cabin.

"What was his hurry?" Two Stars asked when she reached Little Dove.

Talking Bear's eyes locked on Gray Wolf as he entered the Chief's Tepee. Talking Bear could tell from the look on Gray Wolf's face that the news he carried wasn't good.

"Leave us." Talking Bear said to the others as Gray Wolf came and sat down.

Gray Wolf waited until all the other braves had left before he spoke a word.

"The whites by the river have come down with some kind of sickness," he said before falling silent.

"What kind of sickness?" Talking Bear asked.

Gray Wolf watched the fear cover his Chief's face as he said "fever." Talking Bear's face turned pail as he said, "fever?" Making sure he had heard right.

"A few of the whites have already died and there are more getting sick by the day," Gray Wolf went on to say.

Chiefs from the other villages have told them that anyone that tries to leave the camp will die.

"Send a runner to tell the other villages the whites here are under my protection."

Over a hundred braves followed Talking Bear as he left the village. If just one of them had a cold he was going to kill them all.

John and James had just placed the center beam for the house when they noticed Talking Bear and the braves coming.

"Who is that?" James asked.

"I don't know but I'm sure going to find out." John was saying as he climbed down.

Seeing that Talking Bear wasn't wearing war paint was a good sign John thought as he hurried to Adam's side.

"They are not wearing war paint pa." John said as he reached Adam's side.

"I expect I had better go see what this is all about." Adam said as he started toward the Indians.

Adam's heart was pounding hard in his chest and seemed to pound harder with each step he took toward Talking Bear.

Adam felt a bit safer when he heard John say, "I'm coming with you."

"Welcome." Adam said as he stuck out his right hand to Talking Bear. Adam saw that an Indian didn't have to be wearing war paint to be on a war path. Talking Bear paid no attention to Adam's hand and spoke right at John.

"Is anyone sick here?" Talking Bear asked without taking his eyes off John.

Talking Bear saw from the expression on the boy's face that his answer was going to be no.

"Your people by the river have come down with the fever and must be killed to protect our people." Talking Bear said without taking his eyes off John.

"Isn't there something we can do!?" Adam shouted to Talking Bear.

"Yes there is." Talking Bear said as he turned to Adam.

"From now on, no one is to leave this camp, to do so will mean death." Talking Bear pulled back on the horse's leads and backed him up.

"If just one of you tries to leave it will mean the death of you all."

Those were his last words as he rode off. Adam stood in silence and watched as Talking Bear and the braves vanished from sight. Talking Bear turned to Gray Wolf.

"Go and stand guard and if anyone leaves that camp kill them he ordered."

Gray Wolf never said a word he just shook his head and turned his horse toward the woods. By the time Adam and John made it back into camp everyone had gathered just inside the safety of the camp.

"What's going on Master Adam?" George asked as soon as the two reached camp.

John watched and wondered if his pa was going to tell them that for the people by the river this was going to be their last day on earth. Adam looked at John before he spoke.

"No one is to leave this camp for any reason," Adam said once he got them to quiet down. "The people by the river have come down with the fever and Talking Bear said we must stay in camp."

"For how long?" James asked.

Adam turned and said until he tells us different.

It was getting late afternoon and neither John nor Red Hawk had come back yet. That was what Two Stars was thinking as she stared out the window toward the creek.

"So you are finally going to be a mother." Little Dove said as she watched Two Stars staring out the window.

"Yes, I'm sure of it." Two Stars said without even looking at Little Dove. "I wish I could have a baby." Little Dove said as she turned her eyes toward the floor.

Little Dove's words brought Two Starz's eyes back to her best friend not sure she had heard her right.

"You didn't tell me that one of the braves come to you." Two Stars said with excitement.

"Who was it?" Two Stars asked.

"Most of the braves either have someone or they think I'm too old." Little Dove was saying.

"You should do like I did and get you a young stud like John." Two Stars told her.

"What young brave would want me?" Little Dove asked herself and only one name came to her.

John's horse was tied to a tree just inside the camp and when Adam saw John head toward it he ran to stop him. John had just gotten on the horse when Adam grabbed it by the bridle.

"Where do you think you are going?!" Adam yelled.

"I don't think Talking Bear was talking about me." John told him.

"John, he said no one!" Adam yelled again.

Just as John was about to say something an arrow landed in the tree by John's head. John threw himself off the horse to the ground landing with a hard thump.

"I would say that your question was just answered." Adam said trying to see where the arrow had come from.

As soon as John saw the arrow he knew who it belonged too. It was Red Hawk's arrow and if he had wanted John dead he would be. John picked himself up off the ground and dusted off the dirt. John accepted that Talking Bear did mean him. It was almost two weeks before talking bear sent word that John could go back to the cabin and Two Stars. Two Stars walked back and looked out the window to see if John was anywhere to be seen. Not seeing him, she wondered if Talking Bear had gone back on his word to her. He had told her that "if there was still no sickness in the camp he would let John go."

Two Stars was so deep in thought that as she turned her back to the window John appeared.

"Your brother has kept me a prisoner at the camp; were the first words out of his mouth."

"I know." Two Stars said as she put her arms around him. "I hope you understand that he had to protect the people." Two Stars said as she stepped away from John.

"I must admit at first I was angry but the more I thought of the people by the river the more I understood Talking Bear."

Fear crossed Two Star's face when John asked his next question.

"Is there anyone left alive at the river?" He asked.

The look of fear was replaced by a face of stone. The ones that tried to run were killed and the ones that were sick we ended their wait for death. John was glad he was standing right beside the kitchen table and a place to set when his knees grew weak. Two Stars watched as John dropped into the chair and buried his face into his hands. Two Stars came up behind him and placed her hands on his shoulders.

"You must understand he did it for the safety of all the people." She said as she took her hands from John's shoulders and placed them on her belly.

"I know." John said as he raised his head from his hands.

"Are you sure no one got away?" John asked as he rose from the chair.

Two Starz's eyes went from John's to the floor as she answered him.

"Talking Bear's orders were that no one was to be left alive, no one." She said staring at the floor.

Today was the first time Red Hawk had seen Emma come down to the creek without someone with her. He couldn't understand why this slave girl interested him so. Red Hawk watched as Emma's eyes looked for any glimpse of him anywhere.

"Hello." Emma said in a very low voice that if Red Hawk hadn't been close he wouldn't have heard her.

Emma stepped back as Red Hawk seemed to just appear out of nowhere. Even though she expected him his sudden appearance always shocked her. Emma took in a deep breath when Red Hawk did as he always did; took his hand and rubbed it down the side of her face. Emma thought Red Hawk's body looked like it had been carved from stone. His hair was as black as hers and almost as long, it hung down in braids on both sides of his head. She could see that he was older than she was but she didn't care.

"You are no longer frightened of me?" Red Hawk asked as he stopped right in front of Emma.

Emma placed her hands on Red Hawk's shoulders and raised herself on her toes and kissed him. It surprised Emma when Red Hawk jumped back from her like a frightened animal.

"I'm sorry." Emma said as Red Hawk just stood and looked at her. What Emma had done both frightened and excited Red Hawk at the same time.

"Emma!" James yelled from just outside the encampment.

"You must go before you are missed." Red Hawk said pointing toward the camp.

Emma watched as Red Hawk disappeared back into the trees. James caught Emma just as she was entering the camp.

"You know better than to go to the creek all by yourself!" He yelled with anger in his voice.

The sound of James yelling at Emma brought George running to their side.

"I'm sorry Master James I was just getting water."

Red Hawk noticed how Talking Bear motioned for all the other braves to leave as he entered the teepee. Talking Bear told Red Hawk to sit down as soon as the last brave left.

"What did Two Stars tell Little Dove when she stayed with her?" Talking Bear asked.

"Just girl talk is all." Red Hawk said.

"Little Dove told me that Two Stars thinks she may be having a baby is all." Red Hawk went on to say.

Talking Bear's expression looked like he had just been stabbed with a knife.

"What's the matter Talking Bear?" Red Hawk asked not knowing the true meaning of his words.

Talking Bear looked around to make sure they were alone before he spoke.

"If my sister has a male child and I die without one it would become tribal Chief." He said.

"I will not let that happen." Talking Bear said as he jumped to his feet.

"You will not say anything to anyone, do you understand?" Talking Bear ordered at Red Hawk.

Two Stars was jerked awake by the feeling that everything inside her was trying to come out of her mouth. As she opened her eyes everything in the room was out of focus. Just as Two Stars started to get out of the bed her naked body was flung across the bed with her head hung over the side. A smile came to her face as she realized what the meaning of her sickness was. This could only mean one thing she told herself; she was finally going to have a baby. Two Stars was glad that John had gone early and hadn't been there when she got sick. Knowing how John felt about having a child now Two Stars decided to wait until she was showing before telling him. After getting dressed Two Stars went about cleaning up the mess she had just made. As she went about her work she found herself calling out names for boys just to hear what they sounded like. Then she remembered Gold Eagle would name it.

Red Hawk had been ordered to take Little Dove with him and leave her with Two Stars.

Red Hawk knew that Talking Bear was only after as much news as he could get about the baby.

The idea that his Chief was going to such extremes made him frightened for Two Stars.

"Is something wrong brother?" Little Dove asked as she watched Red Hawk deep in thought.

Just as they came to a rock that hung over the path he saw a boy standing pointing a gun at them. Red Hawk had never known fear until the sound of the gun going off rang in his ears. Red Hawk turned just in time to see the bear jumping toward him. The bear hit Red Hawk with such force that it knocked both him and Little Dove off their horses. Red Hawk hit so hard that he was knocked out. James tried to reload the gun but in his excitement the bullets went everywhere. James's heart pounded in his chest as he watched the bear turn his attention to Little Dove. Little Dove laid on the ground frozen in fear watching as the bear came toward her.

Without thinking James through down the gun and pulled out his knife. He placed himself between Little Dove and the bear. The bear's long sharp claws tore hungrily at James's flesh as he tried for the second time to kill the bear. Even though the knife found its mark the second try, the bear was able to get in one more swipe at James before its death.

John had come running to the sound of the gun going off and found his brother down on his knees covered in blood. The first thing Red Hawk saw when he came too was James's knife buried to the hilt into the bear. By the time John reached James he could tell by the blood on the ground that it was bad. Little Dove came and knelt beside James.

"We must take him to the village," she said.

"Why not my cabin?" John asked.

"Do you want this boy to live?" Little Dove asked.

"Yes, of course." John replied.

"Then we will take him to people that can save his life." Little Dove said point blank staring at John.

"Little Dove is right." Red Hawk said as he led his horse to where James could be put on it.

John and Red Hawk walked behind Little Dove as she led the horse with James on it. Just as the horse stopped Red Hawk saw Snow Beaver talking to Little Dove.

"Red Hawk, tell this thing that the boy doesn't have the fever Little Dove ordered once he reached them."

Red Hawk pulled his knife and pointed it at Snow Beaver. "This boy just saved mine and my sister's life if you don't get out of my way I'll kill you where you stand." Red Hawk said.

Snow Beaver knew that Red Hawk meant every word he said. Without a word Snow Beaver backed out of his way. He stood and watched as Little Dove led the horse to her teepee.

John stood in silence and watched as Little Dove went to the place she kept her healing herbs and brought back a small pouch of powder. John watched in amazement as Little Dove mixed it into bear fat-out of all things.

"We must take off his clothing." Red Hawk said to get John's attention. While Little Dove mixed the powder into the bear fat and turned it into paste John and Red Hawk got James undressed. Little Dove picked up the bear fat and a glove maid of mink and came toward him. The only sound that was heard in the teepee was the groans James made as she rubbed the glove over his open wounds. Little Dove could see how John felt; each time the boy cried out he tensed up.

"There is nothing more he can do here." Little Dove said looking at John and talking to Red Hawk.

"You take him out of the way so I can get something done."

Red Hawk took John by the arm and led him out of the teepee.

It wasn't long after the two men had left that James came down with a bad fever. Little Dove was beginning to think that she had took on more than she bargained for. If this boy dies the whites would blame her for his death. Little Dove was glad to see New Crow the village medicine women come in. New Crow had taught Little Dove everything that she knew about healing a broken body. Without a word New Crow walked over and stood looking down at James. New Crow picked up the salve that Little Dove had made up then gave Little Dove a disapproving look.

"Try this instead." The old women said as she pulled out a powder of her own.

"What is that?" Little Dove asked.

"Use it." New Crow said as she handed Little Dove the pouch.

"It is either going to cure him or kill him." New Crow told her with a toothless grin.

Little Dove knew better than to question her.

"He is still young he's got that going for him." New Crow said as she knelt down beside James.

Little Dove respected New Crow not just for her talent for making the sick well but as a mother too. New Crow wasn't her real mother but she had been the only one Little Dove and Red Hawk knew after theirs died.

"The boy saved mine and Little Doves lives," Red Hawk told Talking Bear.

"That is the only reason that he is here but as soon as he can move I want him gone." Talking Bear said pointing at Little Dove's teepee.

The sight of Two Stars riding into the village brought a deep breath from Talking Bear. The way Two Stars handled Talking Bear brought a smile to Red Hawk's face.

"I have come to help Little Dove." Two Stars said as she pushed her way past Talking Bear.

"We'll have the whole white camp here before it's over." Talking Bear was saying as he walked away.

"I don't doubt that." Red Hawk said as he saw him leave.

Red Hawk made his way to a good hiding place very quietly.

John had just reached the white camp to tell them that James was hurt bad. "Have you seen that brother of yours?" Adam asked as John reached him. Adam could see by the way John stared at the ground that he wasn't going to like the answer.

"He's been hurt bad pa he got mauled by a bear." John said before he looked Adam in the face.

"James killed the bear but he got all tore up before he did." "You sure would be proud of him pa he saved Red Hawk and his sister," John said proudly.

"I'll get my horse and we'll go to the village." Adam said as he started to walk off.

"No, pa you can't go to the village." John told Adam as he grabbed Adam by his arm.

"Little Dove even ran me off saying that I was in the way."

"The people at the village can take better care of him than we can." John said.

Adam knew that John was right.

"You know that your maw is going to go if she gets in the way or not." Adam said non-jokingly.

"Yah, I know." John said as he looked toward where the women stood cooking.

"She'll just have to wait until tomorrow, and then we all will go see about James." John told Adam.

"I'll be here at dawn so don't go to the village without me." John said as he got back on his horse and road off.

Adam hadn't noticed that Emma had come up behind him as he watched John ride off.

"Is something wrong Master Adam?" Emma asked when she saw the look on Adam's face.

"Yes Emma its master James, he's been hurt bad but the Indians are taking real good care of him." Adam said.

Adam was just trying out the speech he was going to give Ruth when he told her about James.

"You go find George and tell him that I need him right now." Adam told Emma when he noticed her still standing there.

"Yes Master." Emma said as she ran off in a hurry knowing just where George was.

Liz was helping Ruth set the table when Adam came through the cabin door. She too could tell that there was something very wrong from Adam's face. Liz watched as Adam walked over to the table, pulled out a chair, and told Ruth to sit down.

"Is it John or James?" Ruth asked as she sat down.

"James has been hurt badly by a bear."

Ruth started to say something but Adam stopped her.

"He is alive but the Indians have taken him to their village to care for him."

"I must go to him." Ruth was saying as she came out of the chair.

"Yes, tomorrow we'll go see about him but tonight we stay here." Adam said as he grabbed her by the shoulders to stop her.

Liz became frightened when she couldn't see Emma anywhere. "Master Adam has you seen that silly girl of mine?" Liz asked in a tone that showed her fear.

You could hear the fear leave Liz when Adam told her he had sent her to look for George.

Once Emma had found George and told him what Master Adam had said he left her. Her eyes locked on the half full water bucket then shot straight toward the creek.

"I wonder if Red Hawk is down there." She wondered as she turned back to the bucket.

"I'll bet he will take me to see Master James." Emma told herself as she grabbed up the water bucket and headed for the creek.

Emma thought that she would be frightened to go to the creek by herself but the need to find a way to James overpowered her fear. Red Hawk was surprised to see Emma coming toward the creek without someone with her. He pressed the tip of his fingers to his lips as he remembered the kiss Emma had given him. Emma didn't have to wait long before Red Hawk appeared in front of her.

"I need your help; I want you to take me to see Master James." Emma told him.

"You act like he is a brother instead of your master." Red Hawk said with a confused look on his face.

Red Hawk reached out and grabbed Emma by the shoulders. "He keeps you as a slave and yet you call him brother, it confuses me more than ever."

"I call Master James my brother because that is the way they treat me." Emma said not understanding why Red Hawk couldn't understand that.

"If it hadn't been for Master Adam we all would have been sold off like the others." Emma said.

"Both Master John and Master James treat me as one of the family and I love them for it."

Red Hawk's eyes never left Emma's face as she was talking so he saw she told the truth. Red Hawk thought of how if he was hurt somewhere how Little Dove would date the devil to get to him. What is Talking Bear going to do when he brings the slave girl to the village?

"Please Red Hawk, take me to him." Emma begged as Red Hawk's eyes turned toward the village.

It was late afternoon by the time Red Hawk and Emma reached the village. Red Hawk used the back way in for privacy. James's fever grew higher with each passing hour and Little Dove became increasingly worried with each hour that passed.

"If we dont get his fever down, this boy will be dead by morning. Little Dove said worriedly.

"All we can do now is wait and see what happens. "New Crow said as she gathered up her things to leave.

"You cant leave now; I need you to care for him. "Little Dove said as she stepped in front of New Crowâ€™s path.

"You can take care of him as well as me." New Crow said as she pushed Little Dove aside.

Two Stars rose to her feet and came and stood beside Little Dove.

"We cannot let this boy die." Two Stars said pointing at James.

"That will be decided by the spirits." New Crow said as she pushed Two Stars aside and walked out the door.

Both girls took turns bathing James with a cool wet cloth. It didn't seem to be doing much for James. Emma's heart sank when she saw James's naked body lying lifeless on the pallet. She felt her knees go limp making her fall toward the floor. Two Stars managed to catch her long enough for Red Hawk to take Emma in his arms.

"He's not dead girl." Two Stars said as she threw a blanket over

James's naked body.

Two Stars could see from the look on Emma's face that she had never seen a man naked before.

"Master James, it's me Emma." She said as she took herself from Red Hawk's arms and knelt beside James.

"Master James, you got to get better so's I'll have someone to walk me to the creek." Emma said brushing back tears with each word.

Everyone in the teepee was surprised when James smiled even though he was unconscious. Both Two Stars and Little Dove looked at Emma then at one another.

"Keep talking to him." Two Stars said as she sat down beside Emma just to watch James.

"As long as he can hear you he will fight for life."

Both Ruth and Adam were surprised when George come through the door without knocking.

"Master Adam she's gone, my Emma's gone I can't find her anywhere." George said without stopping.

"Now calm down George she is playing down at the creek I would say." Adam said before seeing that it was dark outside.

"Master Adam, does you think them Indians done took her?" George asked in a worried voice.

"They may have taken her there but I'm sure she isn't in any danger." Adam said to calm George's fears as well as his own.

"Sure, sure, that makes more since; that girl thinks of Master John and Master James more like blood kin." George was saying as he turned and back out the open door without closing it.

"Did you tell George that to ease his fear or yours?" Ruth asked as she came up behind Adam.

"For both of us." Adam said as he walked over and closed the door.

"Do you think they will welcome us?" Ruth asked.

"We're going welcomed or not." Adam told her.

John sat at the table surrounded by darkness except for the light from the lamp in front of him. He thought of going to the village where he knew Two Stars and James were. Then he thought of his pa and knew that he would be going to the village in the morning with or without him. John decided that in the morning would be the best for everyone.

"I'd just as well go to bed." John told himself out loud even though he was the only one there.

John picked up the lamp and headed toward the bed holding the lamp out in front of him. A smile came to John's face as the light of the lamp showed that Two Stars had placed the bear skin on top of the bed. John had finally caught on to what that meant to her. The sight of the empty bed stole the smile from his face. John reached down and pulled back the bear skin blew out the lamp and laid down.

Little Dove sat beside James wiping him with a cool cloth when he started to shiver like he was frozen. She looked at Two Stars and Emma's sleeping bodies to see if James had awakened them. As Little Dove reached over James for a blanket to cover him James threw his arm around her waist and pulled her down on top of him. The noise woke both Emma and Two Stars at the same time. You could see the shock on Emma's face as she saw the Indian woman lying across Master James's naked body. Emma wasn't the only one that was surprised by the sight that greeted them. Two Stars was somewhat surprised by the sight as well.

"He was cold was all." Little Dove said as she reached over and got a blanket to cover James.

Little Dove was glad right then that she was Indian. It helped hide the blushing feeling she felt.

Red Hawk's dreams were of the slave girl and the kiss she had given him at the creek. He also remembered a story that Dan Gains had told him and Talking Bear when they were kids. It was a story about how slave girls could cast a hex on people simply by touching them. Even in his sleep Red Hawk placed his fingers to his lips. Red Hawk was sure she had cast a spell on him because no matter how hard he tried he couldn't get Emma off his mind. Red Hawk's eyes shot open as he sat up in his bed. He thought of Emma being over in Little Dove's teepee just a short distance from him. He quickly put that idea out of his head when he thought of what Talking Bear would do. If Talking Bear found out that he had went against his word he could be thrown out of the village. There is one place that Talking Bear could not stop me from seeing Emma. In my dreams Red Hawk thought as he laid back down.

As soon as the sun had chased the darkness from the sky Adam was ready to go. Adam had put Liz and Ruth in the back of the wagon while he and George rode up front.

"Getty up." George said as he brought the lead rains down on the horse's rumps.

The sound the wagon made when it was jerked into action sounded like a child's cry. Adam looked at the women sitting in the back to see if they had heard it. Seeing that they must not have he turned back to George and winked.

"Miss Ruth, does you think them Indians has done anything to my Emma?" Liz asked.

Ruth took Liz by the hand and patted it on its back.

"No, I'm sure that Emma just went to see about James you know how she feels about him."

The trail to the village had never been made for a wagon so the ride was rough. George pulled the team to a halt when he saw John talking to someone. Snow Beaver wasn't going to let them go in.

As Red Hawk entered Little Dove's teepee the next morning he was surprised at what he seen. Emma was asleep on the ground beside James. The noise that Red Hawk made woke up Two Stars and she saw Red Hawk starring down at the boy. Two Stars got to her feet and stood beside him.

"The boy's fever has broken so he's going to be alright." She said as she came up beside Red Hawk.

Snow Beaver had stopped John from going into Little Dove's teepee and he was getting loud. Two Stars could hear the anger build in John's voice so she ran outside to see what it was about. Red Hawk followed her out and went to Snow Beaver to explain. As soon as Snow Beaver saw Two Stars and Red Hawk come out, he let John by.

"How is he?" John asked as he put his arms around Two Stars and kissed her on the lips.

"He is going to be alright." Two Stars said as she watched Ruth and Liz get out of the wagon.

"Is she here?" Liz asked before reaching her.

"She's in there. "Two Stars said pointing at Little Dove's teepee.

Emma was just getting up as Liz and Ruth walked into the teepee.

"Girl, does you know what you has put me and your pa through?!" Liz yelled as she rushed to her.

Ruth made her way passed Liz and Emma and knelt beside James's sleeping body.

"How did you get here Emma?" Liz asked as she kept her eyes on Red Hawk.

"I made Red Hawk bring me." Emma said pointing at Red Hawk.

Both Two Stars and Little Dove tried not to laugh out loud but the idea that Emma made Red Hawk do anything was funny. Little Dove all the sudden stopped laughing once she thought of the power Emma had over Red Hawk.The puzzle started to fall in to place for why Red Hawk had always been in a hurry all those times. Two Stars saw that Little Dove had stopped laughing and now had a frightened look instead.

"I see that you have met my brother." Little Dove said as she came and stood by Red Hawk's side.

"I can assure you that she was in no danger." Two Stars said in Red Hawk's defense.

Red Hawk didn't need anyone to defend him so he turned and walked out without a word. Red Hawk came out of the teepee just in time to see Talking Bear saying something to Snow Beaver and then Snow Beaver walked away. Talking Bear was asking if Adam and George had come after the boy as Red Hawk reached him.

"How is the boy?" Talking Bear asked and turned to Red Hawk.

"His fever has broken but he is still weak." Red Hawk told Talking Bear then fell silent.

"Little Dove can tell you more." Red Hawk said as they saw Two

Stars and Little Dove headed toward them.

"Will the boy live?" Talking Bear asked once the two girls reached him.

"There she be." George said when he saw Liz and Emma come out of the teepee.

"Can we take the boy home?" Adam asked as he made a jester with his hand toward the teepee.

"No, no, he is much too weak to be moved for at least two days or more." Little Dove said.

"I'm going to take a strap to you when I get you home." George said angrily and grabbed Emma by the arm once she reached him.

"He's not really going to take a whip to her." John said when he saw the anger on Red Hawk's face.

"Why do all your people say things they don't mean?" Red Hawk asked, confused.

John found that he couldn't find a good answer for Red Hawk's question.

"You will leave the boy here but you all must leave." Talking Bear said as he turned and walked away.

Red Hawk walked Emma to the wagon then helped her get in. "Take these people home and I will tell you when he can go." Red Hawk told John.

Both Ruth and Liz watched as Emma stared at Red Hawk as the wagon pulled away. Both knew what her long stare meant. Neither Ruth nor Liz had ever stopped to think about what the young ones would do for mates. The two women stared at each other without saying a word but both knew what the other one was thinking.

The sound of Adam's voice jerked Ruth's thoughts off Emma and back to him. What would she do if something happened to him and she was left alone? Ruth couldn't believe that she hadn't asked herself that question before she came to this wilderness. With all the white men by the river dead by now she would be left to fend for herself.

"Maw, when do you know you love someone?" Emma asked.

Liz fell silent and just kept looking back and forth from Ruth to Emma.

"You're much too young to be worrying about that now." Liz said then turned back to Ruth.

"When it comes time we'll let you know." Ruth said in a voice that said don't ask that again.

Emma looked back at the village without a word.

It was early morning when James woke up in this strange place. He had no idea where he was or how he had gotten there. There was one thing that he was sure of; he wasn't at home in his bed. A sudden pain shot through his shoulder that brought back the memory of the bear attack. James thought he was alone until he saw movement in the darkness. Little Dove had just about fell asleep when she heard James siting up in his bed.

"Are you in pain?" A voice asked from out of the darkness. James could only hear the voice and longed to see who it belonged too. He watched as a small piece of wood seemed to float through the darkness then stopped. Little Dove gently blew on the hot embers and the fire flared a new life. Once the fire came to life it revealed Little Dove's face.

"I must have died." James said in a low voice.

Little dove stuck the flames of the burning stick to the oil lamp that was a gift from Two Stars.

"Are you in pain?" Little Dove asked again once the lamp was lite.

"Just a little but who are you?" James asked when he could see all of Little Dove.

"I'm Little Dove, the women you saved from the bear." She said as she knelt beside James.

"How did I get here?" James asked as he looked around.

"My brother and yours brought you here but you lye back down and rest." Little Dove ordered.

James's face told Little Dove that James was in more pain than he had said. Little Dove reached for a pouch and pulled out some powder to mix in water. She took a dipper full of water and handed it to James.

"Here, drink this it will ease the pain."

"You should be able to sleep now." She went on to say as James drank the water.

After James had laid back down Little Dove picked up and blew out the light.

Even after being told by New Crow that she was going to have a baby Two Stars hid it from John. Two Stars knew how John felt about having a baby and was afraid he would leave her. Two Stars heard John as he came home after working with his pa. Talking Bear had forbid them from going back to the village so John was in a bad mood to start with. I'm going to tell him tonight Two Stars decided as John put up the horse.

"Do you notice anything different?" She asked as John came through the door.

"Yes, you are more beautiful tonight than you were this morning." John said with a smile.

John couldn't understand why what he had said made Two Stars look so mad.

"What about now?" Two Stars asked angrily as she jerked off her dress and stood before John nude.

"Can't you see how big my belly is getting?" She asked as she patted her belly.

"All I can tell you is don't eat so much." John said not seeing what the problem was.

"Would you have me to starve our son?" Two Stars asked.

John jerked back like he had just been shot by a gun. John made his way to the table and pulled out a chair and sat down.

"I'm going to be a father?" John asked.

"Yes you are going to be the father of a tribal Chief someday." Two Stars said proudly.

"Doesn't it have to be a boy for that?" John asked.

"Yes but I know that he will be a strong boy and a strong Chief." Two Stars said as she came up behind John.

"How do you feel?" She asked as she placed her hands on John's shoulders. "It's strange but I really don't know how I feel." John said as he rose from the chair.

Things had went better than Two Stars had hoped so she walked over and laid down on the bear skin on top of the bed. John forgot how tired he was and began taking off his clothing as fast as he could. The sight of her nude body drove John faster.

The next time James opened his eyes was when he felt a cool wet rag touch his body. Once he got adjusted to the light he saw that Little Dove was knelt beside him washing him. The smile quickly left his face when he realized that he was lying there without any clothes on. James reached and grabbed a blanket and pulled it over himself.

"Are you ashamed of your body?" Little Dove asked.

Without a word James shook his head no.

"Then stop acting like a little boy." Little Dove ordered as she continued to wash him.

"I'm young but I'm no little boy." James said in a low voice letting Little Dove wash him.

Little Dove had to smile when James took off the blanket and tossed it aside then rolled over. Little Dove had to admit that for such a young boy he had a large body. When his skin tensed up when she touched it, it gave him the appearance of being made of stone. James closed his eyes and almost fell back to sleep under Little Dove's careful touch. James cracked a smile just before he asked a question.

"Being as now I saved your life does this mean we will get married?" he asked.

Little Dove was tempted to tell him yes but she knew it would not be true.

"No according to tribal law we can't get married if you belong to someone else."

Little Dove could tell by the way James was answering her that he was falling back to sleep.

"There is no one." James said so low that Little Dove could hardly hear him. "What about that slave girl, does she belong to you?" Little Dove asked.

"Do you mean Emma, no I don't own any slaves they belong to my pa." James told Little Dove as he turned back over wide awake.

"Dan Gains used to tell us stories while we sat around the campfire about how white men took the female slaves to bed with them."

"I've known George, Liz, and Emma my whole life. Shoot Liz is like a second mother to me." James told Little Dove.

"Emma is more like a sister than a slave we grew up the same time; to me she is a sister." James went on to say.

"There are slave owners that do take the women to bed but not my pa. We treat our slaves like family that needs to work together to live."

James told Little Dove as he turned back over wide awake.

"Dan Gains used to tell us stories while we sat around the campfire about how white men took the female slaves to bed with them."

"I've known George, Liz, and Emma my whole life. Shoot Liz is like a second mother to me." James told Little Dove.

"Emma is more like a sister than a slave we grew up the same time; to me she is a sister." James went on to say.

"There are slave owners that do take the women to bed but not my pa. We treat our slaves like family that needs to work together to live." told James.

"As long as Emma feels the same way about him it's alright with me James told her."

"I will be sure and tell him that." Little Dove said as she got to her feet to leave.

"Do you have any kids running around here?" James asked with a grin. He had noticed that he hadn't seen any since he woke up.

"No." was all Little Dove said before turning and rushing off.

James couldn't think of what he had said that was wrong.

When Red Hawk stopped by Little Dove's teepee he was surprised to find James awake and sitting up.

"Think you for my sister's life." He told James as he pointed at Little Dove.

"I did it for all of us, that bear didn't care who he had for supper." James said with a laugh.

Little Dove saw something she hadn't seen for a long time; a smile come on Red Hawk's face.

"If you can ride I'll take you home." Red Hawk said as he turned to leave.

Red Hawk was surprised when Little Dove answered for James.

"No, he should stay at least another day or two." Little Dove said as she knelt down beside James.

James looked at Little Dove before he said anything to Red Hawk.

"I don't think I can sit on a horse yet." James said as he laid back down. James propped himself up on one elbow then asked Red Hawk to do him a favor.

"Would you tell John I'm feeling better?" James asked. "Yes." Was all Red Hawk said as he left.

Liz watched as Emma sat staring out the door at the creek. Liz had never thought anything about Emma's love life before now. Out here her only choice now was Master James Liz told herself as she watched Emma. Liz remembered the question Miss Ruth had asked her on the way back from the village. Ruth had asked her what they were going to do if something ever happened to George or Adam. Even now the idea gives her a cold chill. Liz took her long slender finger and brushed back her bangs from her eyes. How did she ever end up here in the middle of nowhere surrounded by a mountain of Indians?All this thinking was starting to give Liz a headache so she went and laid down. She had no more than closed her eyes when Emma was shaking her and asking questions.

"Maw does you think James is getting any better?" Emma asked as Liz opened her eyes.

"It's Master James to you and don't you ever forget it!" Liz yelled loudly. Emma saw anger in her mother's eyes as she stared into them.

Not knowing what had made her maw so mad Emma backed away from her.

"Is you asking about Master James as a sister or something else?" Liz asked.

"Yes, it's because I think of…" Emma paused before going on.

"It's because Master James is like a brother to me maw." Emma told Liz.

"It's not like we were getting married or anything." Emma said as she turned her back toward the door.

"I love Master James but not like that." Emma said without looking at Liz.

Emma looked and saw that the water bucket were half full and frowned. A quick glance to see that Liz wasn't watching Emma walked over and accidently kicked the bucket over spilling all the water. George sat at the table and looked up to see what all the noise was about.

"Now you go fetch some more water!" George yelled at Emma.

Two Stars rolled over and found her nose right in the middle of John's beard. The idea still amazed her how a white hair grew on his face. She really didn't like it but it was his face. Each time John took a breath the hair of John's beard would tickle Two Stars' nose. Two Stars eased her way out of bed so she wouldn't disturb John. As Two Stars watched, a smile came to John's face in his sleep. I wonder if he is dreaming of me and the baby Two Stars asked herself.

"Should I wake him and get him gone before the morning sickness sets in." Two Stars asked herself.

It would be best to keep such things away from him she had told herself. Two Stars bent over to pick up her dress off the floor where she had dropped it the night before.

"Are you sick?" John asked as Two Stars started putting on the dress. "Maw told me that women get sick in the mornings." John said as he too got dressed.

Once Two Stars had gotten dressed she turned to watch John dress. She watched as he pulled his buck skin pants up over his muscular legs. Next he took the shirt she had made him and pulled it down over his broad shoulders. He was just a boy a few months ago now he was a man about to be a father. This man was better than her wildest dreams Two Stars told herself.

"Do you want me to stay here with you instead of going to the village?" John asked as he put on the last boot.

Just as Two Stars was about to tell John no she got the sudden need to run for the door shaking her head no. John was kind enough to wait for Two Stars to finish her morning thing before asking her anymore questions. Two Stars took the back of her hand and wiped her mouth before she spoke.

"Do you want to go with me to the village?" John asked her once she finished wiping her mouth.

Liz waited until Emma had left before she said anything to George.

"George has you ever thought about where Emma's going to find a husband out here in the middle of nowhere?" Liz asked him.

"What is you getting at women?" George asked very loudly.

Liz pulled out the other chair and sat down beside George.

"I think she has got her eyes on an Indian boy." George said.

"See that's what I mean, what if she wants to marry up with that Indian?" Liz asked.

"You telling me Emma wants to marry that Indian?" George said then laughed.

"Master Adam won't let Emma marry an Indian." George told Liz once he stopped laughing.

"Master Adam thinks of Emma as the girl he never had." George said.

"That's my point George, Emma is either going to marry up with an Indian or Master James." Liz told him.

"At least with the Indian she will be free." Liz said. "I tell you Master Adam will not let Emma go free to an Indian; he wouldn't even if she was white."

"We are treated well by Miss Ruth and Master Adam but are still slaves don't forget it." Liz said.

"How can I forget anything like that?" George yelled angrily. "Do you think it was my idea to bring us here to this jungle?" George said as he made a jester with his arm toward the outside.

"Tell you the truth, I'd rather be on a nice tobacco plantation where you didn't have to worry about being killed every day." George said as he rose to leave.

"Besides Master Adam won't let one of his kids marry up with an Indian." George was saying as he went out the door.

"What about the Indian that's married to Master John?" Liz asked when he was too far to hear her.

At least with the Indian she would be free Liz said more to herself than anyone. Liz watched as George headed toward the creek talking to himself.

George said, "I'm going to put an end to this."

Emma looked up and down the creek bed and expected Red Hawk to appear out of nowhere. When he didn't show up she knelt down and dipped the bucket in the water. Emma noticed how the ripples caused by the bucket broke up her reflection on the water. When all the ripples had gone and the water regained its mirrored surface again she saw it. Her reflection showed an Indian behind her and it wasn't Red Hawk. Emma became so frightened that when she jumped up she lost her footing and fell into the creek.

"You don't need to fear me." Talking Bear said as he stuck out his hand to help Emma up.

"I have sent Red Hawk to do something else he won't be back for a while." Talking Bear said without changing the expression on his face.

"I'z sorry Master but you frightened me." Emma told Talking Bear as he helped her up.

"Do not call me Master; in my land everyone is free." Talking Bear said when Emma reached him.

Talking bear saw that Emma wasn't hurt just wet. "I'z sorry Master if my foolish girl is bothering you." George said as he reached them.

"I'm not your Master." Talking Bear said angrily before turning and walking off.

"Girl you gets that water and get to the house." George ordered Emma as he watched Talking Bear leave.

Emma knew that her pa was mad and she was more afraid of what George was going to do to her than she had been of Talking Bear.

Adam stood out on his porch when he saw Emma running toward their cabin with a bucket of water spilling out both sides as she ran.

"Silly girl must have fallen in the creek." Adam told himself when he saw Emma's wet dress.

It wasn't until he saw George coming behind her that Adam knew something was wrong.

"What's going on George?" Adam asked as he walked out to catch him. "It's that foolish girl of mine Master Adam, she been meeting that Indian boy down at the creek."

"Liz, say they want to marry up but I sat her straight I told her you wouldn't let her Master."

Two Stars was glad that John had gone for the day and she was left alone with the baby.

She had gotten over her morning sickness and was about to clean the cabin. As she did the cleaning she thought of how much she had fallen in love with John. The next thought jerked the smile from Two Starz's face. It seemed that through the past when Two Stars was the happiest was when bad things started. She wasn't living the life she had always dreamed about as a girl when she was given to Dan Gains. John was as different as night and day from Dan. That was what frightened her so much the power he held over her. Two Stars had already accepted that for her to keep John she would have to accept his family. She found them strange but likable.

The sound of Red Hawk calling her sent Two Stars running to the porch.

"You headed to see that slave girl?" Two Stars asked laughingly.

The smile didn't appear that Two Stars expected. Red Hawk didn't feel much like laughing at Two Starz's silly question after what Talking Bear said. He had been ordered by Talking Bear not to see the slave girl again.

"I was sent to stay here and see that you and the baby come to no harm." Red Hawk told her.

"You can tell my brother that my husband is already doing that when you get back." She said.

Two Stars wasn't surprised when Red Hawk went ahead and got off his horse anyway. Two Stars knew that she would be wasting her breath to say anything to him about not staying. Once Talking Bear had given Red Hawk an order he was going to obey it no matter what.

"Do you want to come in?" Two Stars asked knowing what the answer was going to be.

Two Stars never could figure out why Red Hawk would never enter her cabin. Even as a boy when he came to see her and Dan he would never come inside. To find out what Talking Bear thought about her baby, Red Hawk would know best Two Stars told herself as she walked to him.

Emma could tell that George was angry as she watched him come through the door.

"Did that Indian touch you girl?" George asked angrily.

"No pa he just surprised me and I fell in is all." Emma told George.

"Your maw's been telling me you been meeting an Indian boy down at the creek." He shouted.

"I'm going to tell you right now that it is over with him. Do you understand?" George asked her.

"From now on you will not go to the creek without me." George said in a softer tone.

"I should take the strap to you for your own good." George said pointing at the razor strap hanging on the wall.

"Now George you get out of here and let her get out of them wet things." Liz said as she hurried George out the door.

"Girl if you don't stay away from that Indian boy you is going to get us all killed." Liz said as she handed Emma a dry dress to put on.

"Red Hawk is his name." Emma said staring out.

John thought it strange that James wasn't ready to come home yet. To John he looked like he was healthy enough to ride a horse to paw's he thought. As Little Dove walked John to the door he looked back at James and swore he winked at him.

"Tell Two Stars that if she ever needs me just send word by Red Hawk." She told John at the door.

"I will tell her what you said." John told her as he went out the door.

The second surprise came when John saw Talking Bear standing at his horse. "I have sent Red Hawk to stay with Two Stars to protect her and the baby." Talking Bear said as John reached him.

"It is my job to protect Two Stars and my baby." John said calmly as he mounted his horse.

"The first thing I'm going to do is send Red Hawk back to the village when I get home."

"Two Stars is the daughter of a tribal Chief and she is one of the people; I will protect her as a sister." Talking Bear said.

"She is of my people now that she is carrying my baby." John said as he kicked the horse forward.

Talking Bear didn't have any respect for John the boy, but he found respect for John the man.

Respect or not Talking Bear wasn't going to let him taunt the people's blood with that white blood. If Two Starz's baby was a girl it would be no threat but if it was a boy then it must die before it lives. Talking Bear stood and watched as John rode away. A smile came to Talking Bear's face as he thought of John trying to run Red Hawk off. If John gets Red Hawk mad enough he will solve my problem for me Talking Bear thought.

Little Dove stood at her teepee door and saw Talking Bear turn and walk away smiling. She had no idea what it was all about but it was something that gave her a cold chill. She couldn't remember seeing Talking Bear do that before and it frightened her. As Little Dove stood looking out the door James grew curious as to what she was looking at.

"What are you looking at?" James asked as he slowly made his way to his feet.

"You should stay off your feet." Little Dove said as she guided James back to the bed.

"It was nothing but Talking Bear walking by." Little Dove told James as he laid back down.

"Is there something wrong with me being here?" He asked as Little Dove turned back toward the door.

Little Dove turned back to James before saying anything.

"You saved mine and Red Hawk's lives so you will always be welcomed in my teepee." She said.

"Now you must rest." Little Dove said then got to her feet.

She couldn't understand what it was about this boy that attracted her so. The way he brought out feelings in her that she thought were buried a long time ago. Or was it that Two Stars had gotten the baby that both girls had wanted.

"Why did Talking Bear send you here?" Two Stars asked as she sat down by Red Hawk. The place that Red Hawk had chosen to sit was under the shade of a tall pine tree.

"Talking Bear knows about the baby so he sent me here to help you." Red Hawk said without looking at Two Stars.

Tribal law calls for all the people to safe guard the life of a future Chief Two Stars remembered. She had been sure that Talking Bear would resent the baby. Had she misjudged her brother; was he concerned about her baby?

"Two Stars, what do you think about the slave girl?" Red Hawk asked without looking at her.

Red Hawk wasn't looking at Two Stars or he would have seen the smile that came to her face.

"I find her different than the white people." Two Stars said as she lost her smile.

"You must realize that the whites don't look at her as we do." "To the whites she is their property and not free." Two Stars said trying to explain to him.

"Is we going to the village this morning Master Adam?" George asked as he approached him.

"I was thinking about it seeing as how John has been the only one aloud to see James for weeks."

"Speaking of the John there he is." Adam said as John came into view.

"Have you seen James?" Adam was asking even before John got the horse stopped.

"Yes pa, I've seen him and he is feeling well." John said then looked toward the village and laughed.

"Master John, you is going to half to give that girl of mine a talking to." George was saying as John got down from his horse.

"What is he talking about pa?" John asked not taking his eyes off George.

"Emma has been seeing an Indian boy down by the creek." Adam said as he joined John in looking at George.

"You know the one that always ride's on Talking Bears right." He said.

"That's Red Hawk he is a good choice." John said to the amazement of both Adam and George.

"Did you think she was going to marry me?"

"To tell you the truth I've never stopped to think about it." Adam told John. "Emma is like your sister and she wants to marry up with an Indian." George said loudly.

"That's my point pa; Emma is like a sister instead of a slave to me and James. we could never marry her."

"Then you want me to sat her free?" Adam asked.

John laughed as he pointed out at the trees and said, "What will she do with her freedom out here pa?"

George could feel the chains of slavery fall to the ground as John spoke. George decided not to say anything to spoil this feeling just in case he woke up and found it was all a dream.

"I was thinking of going to the village today and seeing about James." Adam said as he faced John.

"No pa you had better not go there." John told Adam as John tied the horse. "The Indians don't want us there and Talking Bear is just looking for an excuse to do the same thing he did to them by the river."

Adam didn't like it but he knew John was right.

Two Stars had enjoyed spending the day with Red Hawk; she missed the old days like this. Red Hawk had caught two large fish and now he sat under his shade tree while she cleaned them. As Two Stars looked to see if Red Hawk was still under the tree she saw John ride in. When she saw John stop his horse right where Red Hawk was sitting, the grin left her face. She could tell that there was something wrong by the way John was acting.

"Red Hawk I have been told by Talking Bear that you were sent here to protect Two Stars and the baby. Now I will tell you like I told him, I do not need your help protecting my family." John told him.

Red Hawk could hear the anger in John's voice even though he tried to hide it.

"I was not sent here for you I was sent here for the life of a tribal Chief."' Red Hawk said as he got to his feet.

"I was sent here to do the lifting for Two Stars." Red Hawk went on to say once he was on his feet.

John was just about to say something to Red Hawk when Two Stars reached them.

"John, I'm glad you are home I was just fixing to cook the fish Red Hawk caught for us." She said.

John's bright blue eyes looked straight into Red Hawk's dark ones. "I see what you mean by help for Two Stars." John said as he turned to her. "You can come to the cabin and wait John told Red Hawk as he headed for the cabin."

"No." Red Hawk said as he took a step back from John and Two Stars. John kept looking over his shoulder at Red Hawk as he followed Two Stars to the cabin.

"Why won't Red Hawk come into the cabin?" John asked as he

followed Two Stars through the door.

"To tell you the truth I don't know, I don't really know." Two Stars said as she looked back at Red Hawk sitting under the tree again.

"He has been like that from the time he was a little boy." Two Stars said as she went inside.

Strange John thought as he too went inside.

James laid in the darkness and wondered if Little Dove was awake as well. He thought of making his way over and lying down beside her but soon disregarded the idea.

"She might take it wrong and kill me before she knew who it was." James told himself.

James heard movement from the darkness in the direction that Little Dove laid.

"Light the lamp so I can see you." James said as she got closer.

"No." Was the word Little Dove replied as she reached James's side.

"I want you to pretend that I am one of your slave girls and take me like one." She said.

Little Dove was surprised when James broke into a big laugh. Little Dove I have never taken a slave girl or a white girl in my life James told her.

"You mean you are a virgin?" Little Dove asked not knowing if the question would be answered.

When James shook his head yes it both excited and frightened Little Dove. He reached and got her by the arm and pulled it.

"I will pretend to be whatever you want." James said as he pulled Little Dove toward him.

James was glad that Little Dove had not lite the lamp because he felt himself blush. Thinks to the darkness Little Dove could not see him. Little Dove was also glad for the darkness because it hid from her that the man she was making love to was still a boy. For a virgin James was a fast learner Little Dove thought as her own passion exploded. Little Dove collapsed on top of James's chest with her ear lying on his heart.

"Was I good Master James?" Little Dove said with a laugh.

"Shouldn't I be asking that question?" James said with a laugh of his own. James turned Little Dove to him and kissed her. She had found the act of kissing as strange as Red Hawk did at the creek. James's eyes had grown adjusted to the darkness to where he could see Little Dove's face. She told him she had never kissed before.

Both Little Dove and James laid naked as Red Hawk walked in the next morning. Little Dove wasn't sure if what she was seeing was real or not until she saw the look on Red Hawk's face. She quickly set up and reached for her dress trying to decide if her anger at Red Hawk was because he just walked in or because she was caught. Little Dove's fast movements caused James to wake up with Red Hawk staring down at him. James could also tell that from the look in Red Hawk's black eyes he didn't like what he saw. The look on James's face would have been funny if it wasn't so serious.

"I come to see if he was well enough to go back to the camp I see that I don't have to ask that question!" Red Hawk yelled.

"And you I may owe you my life but I will not see my sister turned into a red slave!" Red Hawk yelled at James without lowering his voice.

"It's not like that." James was saying as he put on his pants as fast as his shoulder would let him.

There was one thing that Two Stars and Little Dove had in common, a large temper.

"I have you know that this is still my teepee and I'll bed who ever I want!" Little Dove yelled back.

James was just as surprised as Red Hawk at Little Dove's outburst.

Just as Red Hawk started to say something else he heard Talking Bear calling his name. After a look at Little Dove and telling her that this wasn't over he turned and walked out. As Red Hawk walked toward Talking Bear he asked himself if he should tell him of what he saw in Little Dove's teepee. Before he reached Talking Bear he had decided that it would only cause trouble for Little Dove.

"Can the boy be moved?" Talking Bear asked as Red Hawk approached where he and Snow Beaver stood.

"Yes, he is doing well today." Red Hawk said as he looked toward James as he came out of the teepee and stood talking to Little Dove.

Talking Bear said "Good." then sent Snow Beaver to bring two horses as fast as he could.

"I'll make them let you stay." Little Dove said.

"No, it's time for me to go." James said as he saw Red Hawk coming their way.

"I owe you my life." James said as he squeezed Little Dove's hand and walked to meet Red Hawk.

Both James and Red Hawk stood in silence as they waited for Snow Beaver to bring the horses. James rode behind Red Hawk on their way back to the camp. It got to where James couldn't stand the silence no more so he spoke up.

"I do not think of Emma as a slave and I sure don't think of Little Dove that way." He said.

Red Hawk stopped his horse so James could catch up with him. "I will not have you treat my sister like you do the slave girl, Emma." Red Hawk said as James caught up with him.

"How many times do I got to tell you that Emma is not my slave?" James asked.

"That is my point she does not belong to you she belongs to your father." Red Hawk told James.

"Your pa holds Emma's life in his hands not you."

James had never stopped to think about it before but Red Hawk was right only his pa could give Emma her freedom. James sped his horse up until he regained his place beside Red Hawk.

"I will get my pa to let Emma go free if you will believe that I love Little Dove." James said as he rode beside Red Hawk.

"That will do no good, I have been ordered by Talking Bear to stay away from her." He said.

That seemed like a strange order to James but everything about these Indians was strange to him.

Red Hawk rode the rest of the way to John's cabin in silence and alone.

"I will leave you here." Red Hawk said as James reached where he had stopped his horse.

"I will see what I can do for Emma I give you my word." James said as he rode on passed Red Hawk.

James could see the mistrust in Red Hawk as he headed on toward the camp. Winning Red Hawk's trust wouldn't be easy.

Liz and Ruth were busy preparing the evening meals as James rode into camp. Ruth had her back to him so Liz saw him first.

"Oh, Master James!" Liz said as she through her arms into the air and ran toward James.

As Ruth turned around Liz was almost too where James had stopped the horse.

"My baby." Ruth said in a low voice as she dropped the pan she was holding to the ground.

"James is it really you?" Ruth said as she wrapped her arms around James and pulled him to her.

The door to George's cabin came open and Emma stepped out.

"Master James!" Emma yelled as she too ran to greet him home.

Adam and George had been sitting at the table talking when Emma had yelled Master James and ran out. Both men rose to their feet and hurried out to make sure they had heard Emma right. Both broke into a big smile when they saw that Emma was right. They all followed him as he went inside.

By the time James reached his bed he was ready to put it to good use. By the time he got stretched out on the bed he realized the room was full of people. It seemed to James that they all were asking different questions for him to answer. James answered as many of the questions as he could then he noticed Emma standing in the back not saying a word.

"Why is my sister not saying welcome?" James asked as he held out a hand to her.

The cabin suddenly went quiet and every eye went to Emma who stood frozen speechless.

"I came to the village Master James." Emma was finally able to say.

"Yes they told me at the village that you were there." James told her.

"It was my pleasure Master James." Emma said then smiled.

"From now on just call me James." He went on to say.

Both George and Liz looked at each other but said nothing.

"Now everyone out of here and let this boy get some rest." Ruth ordered as she hurried them toward the door.

George got Emma by the arm as she came out the door. "Girl you gets yourself to the cabin and stay there." George ordered before he let go of her arm.

"Master Adam, I'z sorry about that Emma she is always getting into things." George said.

"She just doesn't realize all the danger she may be putting us in." Adam said as he stepped off the porch.

It wasn't her that brought us here; George thought as he stepped off behind Adam.

Ruth waited until everyone had gone before she spoke to James. "James you shouldn't have told Emma not to call you Master in front of everyone." Ruth said with a jester of her hand toward George's cabin.

"But maw, Emma is like a sister I don't think of her as a slave." James told Ruth.

Maybe changing his pa's and maw's thinking on slavery wasn't going to be as easy as he thought. As James laid there with his eyes closed he asked himself if he had made a promise to Red Hawk that he couldn't keep.

It has been almost a month since James had gone back to his people. Little Dove set in her empty teepee thinking of how much she missed having James to talk to. The sound of someone coming up to her door brought a smile to her face as she hurried to see who it was. The sight of Talking Bear standing there soon took the smile from her face. There was something different about the way Talking Bear was acting that bothered her. Any other time Talking Bear just came out and said what was on his mind today he stood silent for a while before he spoke. My sister sent Red Hawk back to the village and will not let him stay. Talking Bear fell silent and looked around before talking in a low voice even though she and Talking Bear were the only ones there.

"I want you to go to her and make her let you stay."

"I have already told Two Stars that anytime she needed me to send word by Red Hawk. She has never sent me word yet." Little Dove found herself saying.

"I need you to do it for the people as well as Two Starz's sake." Talking Bear said in a tone that told Little Dove it was an order.

"I will be glad to go stay with Two Stars until the baby is born." She said as she began getting her things together for her trip.

"You cannot tell my sister that I sent you; do you understand?" Talking Bear asked.

"I promise that I won't say a word." Little Dove told him as she went about getting ready to go.

Talking Bear shook his head and walked out. Little Dove's smile returned with the thought of staying with Two Stars and John. Of course if she was there she was sure that James would come by every day she thought.

"Could she get as lucky as Two Stars had and have a baby at her age?"

She wanted a baby no matter who fathered it.

John had been spending most of his time working for Adam in the daytime and with Two Stars at night. James was well enough now that he was helping John today. John watched as James stopped what he was doing and just stared at the path that led to the village.

"What can you tell me about Indian women?" James asked without taking his eyes off the path.

When James turned to face John he saw that John was smiling and pulling off his gloves.

"It's too hot here to talk about Little Dove." John said as he headed for a shade tree.

"You know about her?" James asked.

He didn't think anyone knew but him, Little Dove, and Red Hawk. "Sure I know, Two Stars told me a few days after it happened." John told him.

"Look little brother I'm not the one you should be asking these questions; you should be asking Two Stars." John said then smiled.

"No, I couldn't tell Two Stars how I feel about Little Dove."

"You know, John I think Little Dove cast a spell on me when I was there." James said.

"There hasn't been a single night that she hasn't been in my dreams."

John laughed out loud.

"The spell she cast on you is more powerful than any black magic." John said laughingly.

"How does Little Dove feel about you?" John asked once he stopped laughing.

"I think she likes me too but her brother Red Hawk doesn't think much of it." James said.

"I'm not sure how Little Dove feels about me; I haven't seen her since I left the village."

"The only way to know how Little Dove feels about you little brother is to ask Two Stars." John was saying as he rose to his feet.

"You come with me to the cabin tonight and then you can ask Two Stars your questions." John told James as he walked off.

"How could I talk to Two Stars about sex if I can't talk to Little Dove about it?" James was asking as he got to his feet as well.

James hurried to catch John and the days end.

Red Hawk and twenty braves had been sent by Talking Bear to the river to make sure there were no whites or slaves left alive. His instructions were to kill everyone then burn everything. Red Hawk stopped the braves just outside the camp and started going in by himself. Snow Beaver started to follow Red Hawk but Gray Wolf called him back. The smell of death was so bad that Red Hawk started breathing through his mouth. Red Hawk went back to the braves and ordered them to burn everything while he rode around making sure they hadn't missed any cabins. As Red Hawk stopped at a creek to get a drink he found something that shouldn't have been there. Red Hawk quickly rose to his feet and his keen eyes searched for the slightest movement. After not seeing anything his eyes went back to the small footprint right in front of him. The print had to be a child's print because it was so small. Red Hawk tied his horse and followed the tracks up the hill to a darkened bear cave. Knowing that he was going to need light inside, Red Hawk built a fire and placed a large piece of wood in it for a torch. Once it started burning good he picked it up and went inside. The darkness made it hard for Red Hawk to see even with a torch held out in front of him. As he neared the back of the cave he found the body of a grown women lying there. Just as Red Hawk was about to turn and leave he heard a noise in the darkness. As Red Hawk tried to see what had made the noise a large rock hit him in the head knocking him to the ground. Red Hawk couldn't believe what he saw next as a very young child ran past him and out of the cave. The rock had cut Red Hawk above the eye and the blood was blinding him. He thought that catching a little girl shouldn't be too hard but found out how wrong he was.

Rose Marie was fast and may have gotten away if she hadn't went the wrong way and gotten trapped. Rose found herself caught between two large hills and the only way out was past a very mad and bleeding Indian. As Rose stood and watched Red Hawk coming toward her she remembered watching with her mother how the Indians had killed everyone. She also remembered how her mother had brought her to the cave when people started getting sick. Her mother had died from a snake bite she got two days ago. The sound of Red Hawk brought Rose's attention back to him. Red Hawk stopped and looked at Rose out of the eye that wasn't swelled shut.

The fact that Red Hawk said," I'm not going to hurt you." In perfect English didn't stop her from reaching down and picking up another rock.

"I can take you to the whites." Red Hawk said as he stopped where he was.

"Wait, I can help you." Red Hawk said as Rose drew back the rock to throw. Red Hawk kept his good eye on the hand that held the rock as he talked to Rose. Rose had heard the words white people and asked herself if she should trust Red Hawk. She stood and watched as Red Hawk took off his bow and arrows and lied them on the ground. Only after Red Hawk had stepped away from the bow and arrows did Rose let the rock fall from her hand. Red Hawk took a breath of relief as the rock hit the ground. Red Hawk saw Rose's eyes light up when he told her that he would take her to Emma. Rose came toward Red Hawk a few feet then stopped in her tracks. Red Hawk picked up his bow and arrows and led the way out. With his back to her Rose couldn't see the smile on Red Hawk's face. Rose kept her distance from Red Hawk but followed him all the way back to the horse.

Two Stars was really showing now so she was letting out her dresses so they would fit her. She had stopped having morning sickness and it was replaced by the need to eat everything. On this warm day Two Stars had left the cabin door open so the breeze could blow in. Two Stars had always loved this time of year when the leaves begin changing color and falling to the ground. Two Stars jumped to her feet and ran to the door when she heard a horse outside.

"Maybe John is coming home early today." She told herself as she hurried to the door.

Two Starz's eyes stopped and looked at the knife as she headed for the door. Deciding that it wasn't any need for it she let it hang where it was as she went outside. She could tell from the direction the horse was coming that it was from the village. Maybe it's Red Hawk Two Stars thought as she still couldn't see who it was yet.

"At least it will be someone to talk to." She told herself as she went out onto the porch.

A smile crossed Little Dove's face as the cabin came into view. The sight of Two Stars standing on the porch made her smile grow larger. Little Dove saw that Two Stars had her back to her so she stopped the horse and went the rest of the way through the woods. Two Stars kept looking toward the path but no one had appeared. She watched the path so hard that she didn't see Little Dove come up behind her.

"You have been spending way too much time with that white boy." Little Dove said from behind Two Stars.

Two Stars knew who it was before she turned around and hugged her friend.

"Look at you; you're getting so big." Little Dove said as she stepped back and looked Two Stars over.

"How is the little Chief doing?" Little Dove asked as she placed a hand on Two Starz's belly.

"I think he is in a hurry to get out because yesterday he kicked me so hard it hurt. Come on in we have a lot of catching up to do."

It wasn't until Two Stars started back into the cabin that she noticed how much stuff Little Dove had brought with her. Two Stars started to ask Little Dove what it was all about then decided she would tell her when she was ready.

"We have so much to catch up on." Two Stars said as she led Little Dove through the door.

"I have come to help you with the next little Chief." Little Dove said as she followed Two Stars in.

"Is that why you brought your things?" Two Stars asked. Little Dove knew that her best friend had already caught on to why she was there. Little Dove made sure that she was looking Two Stars in the eyes before she spoke.

"Your little brother sent me here because the boy won't let Red Hawk stay." Little Dove said not taking her eyes off of Two Starz's eyes.

Two Stars knew that what Little Dove was telling her was the truth by the way she looked her in the eyes.

"My home is your home." She said then smiled. "Where is that old man of yours?" Little Dove asked as she joined Two Stars at the table.

"Oh he hasn't made it home yet." Two Stars told her as she saw her friend staring out the door. "Come on James." John said as he reached out a hand to help James onto the horse.

"I think I should have washed off before seeing Two Stars." James said as he climbed up behind John.

"I know a good place close to the cabin where we can both wash."

John said as he kicked the horse to get him started.

Two Stars and Little Dove talked as they went about cooking John a big supper for when he got there. Two Stars was surprised when Little Dove told her about the night before James left the village. Two Stars wasn't going to let Little Dove see the shock she felt inside.

"They sure are a strange people." Two Stars said then laughed.

"I think John is coming." Two Stars said as she rose from her chair.

The sound she was hearing was coming from the creek but it wasn't getting any closer.

"What do you think it is?" Little Dove asked as she joined Two Stars at the door.

"It's coming from where John and I take our bathes." Two Stars told Little Dove as she smiled and shoved her out the door.

"It sounds like there is someone with him." Two Stars said as she headed toward the creek.

Two Stars saw that the noise she was hearing was the sound of two boys playing in the water. As Two Stars started to turn around and head back to the cabin Little Dove grabbed her by the arm and pulled her down behind a bush.

"What are you doing?" Two Stars asked as she too sat behind the bush that hid them from view.

"Let's watch the boys be boys." Two Stars said as she pulled back a limb on the bush so she could see better.

The first thing that Little Dove noticed was how close the boys had left their clothes to her. Two Stars knew what her friend was thinking when she saw her smile and head for them.

"No!" Two Stars yelled at Little Dove as she reached for the boys clothes. Little Dove waited until both boys had their backs to her then grabbed them up and hurried back into the bushes. Little Dove was laughing so loud that Two Stars was sure she was going to be heard. Little Dove stopped laughing when she saw that her best friend didn't find it as funny as she did.

As John turned he could see that their clothes weren't where they were supposed to be.

"Where is our clothes John?" James asked as he to saw them gone. "Did some wolf carry them off?" He asked.

"Not unless he can walk on two legs." John told James as he stood where the clothes use to be.

James could see what John was talking about when he joined him on the bank. Little Dove had been quiet enough but she had left her foot prints everywhere. Both boys turned around when they heard the sound of a horse behind them. Both of them froze as they saw who was coming.

"Come child I'll take you to the white people." Red Hawk said and stuck out his hand for Rose to take.

Rose didn't take Red Hawk's hand but stood staring up at him from beside the horse. Rose thought of how it had been in that cave, alone, at night before she let Red Hawk put her on the horse. It wasn't but a few seconds after he had got Rose seated in front of him when he saw two of the braves headed toward him. At the same time he watched the trust he had built between him and Rose disappear as well. Red Hawk thought of the orders he had been given by Talking Bear before he left. He had been told to burn everything and kill everyone left alive. Red Hawk was sure the child didn't have the sickness from the way she acted. Both Gray Wolf and Snow Beaver looked at each other as Red Hawk rode by them with the child in front of him. Neither one said a word as he rode past them. It had been a long ride from the river for both Red Hawk and Rose. She had grown used to having him behind her and sat quietly without moving. Rose could tell that it was getting late in the afternoon from the setting sun. Just as the horse came around a corner there standing on the creek bank was two naked men. Rose screamed and jumped from the moving horse and ran.

"Not again." Red Hawk said as he too jumped from the horse and began chasing Rose for the second time that day.

The sound of a little girl's scream coming from the creek bed caught both Two Stars and Little Doves attention. Little Dove dropped the bundle of clothes she was carrying and ran toward the sound. Two Stars wanted to run as well but first she had to stop and pick up the boys clothing before she could go. As Little Dove reached where the boys stood they tried to hide themselves from her. As Two Stars reached where the two boys stood trying to hide themselves, John raised his hand long enough to point out the direction the others had ran.

"She went this way." Little Dove said when Two Stars reached her. "What is going on?" Two Stars asked not knowing who or what they were after.

"I really don't know but from the look on Red Hawk's face it was going to be trouble." Little Dove said before she started running again.

Rose had stopped to catch her breath when she spotted smoke coming from the top of the hill in front of her. The sound of Red Hawk getting closer and now the sound of more people drove Rose up the hill. Emma was getting more fire wood for the night when she saw Rose run into camp. As soon as Rose saw Emma she knew she was safe enough to let her tears flow. Ruth and Liz both looked at each other just to make sure the other had seen it to. A white child had just run straight to Emma.

"Rose Marie is that you?" Emma asked not sure she wasn't seeing a ghost.

Rose didn't take time to answer her she just ran and threw her arms around Emma. Rose had remembered Emma from the trail out here. Emma had let Rose walk with her and the two had talked about everything even her pa.

"Get yourself away from that girl Emma." George said as his big hand clamped to Emma's shoulder and jerked her little friend.

Emma hit the ground so hard that it knocked the breath out of her.

"You can't touch her child." Adam said as he reached them.

Rose fell to her knees crying and shaking her head from side to side. Tears poured from both of Rose's eyes because the people she thought would help her were going to turn her away. As soon as the tears let her see again Rose saw Red Hawk enter the camp. Rose got to her feet and watched as he got closer. Red Hawk saw Rose rise to her feet and he thought he was going to have to chase her again. To everyone's surprise Rose walked to him and put out her arms.

"Don't touch her!" Adam yelled as Red Hawk knelt down and took Rose in his arms.

"This child doesn't have the sickness." Red Hawk assured them.

"How do you know that?" Adam said as he reached Rose and Red Hawk. Red Hawk rose to his feet and looked Adam in the eyes before he spoke.

"Because the ones with the sickness died weeks ago." Red Hawk said angrily.

Both Two Stars and Little Dove were out of breath by the time they reached the camp.

"What's the matter with you Adam?" Ruth asked as she went past him and took Rose into her arms and carried her into the cabin.

"Girl you fetch some water and give her a bath." Liz told Emma as they followed Ruth in.

Red Hawk decided he had just about enough of the whites for one day and left.

"Do you need a ride Little Dove?" Red Hawk had asked just before he left.

"No I'll be staying with Two Stars." She said as she watched John's reaction to what she said.

"I've told James he could stay the night." John said looking at Two Stars.

"We can make room for both." Two Stars said as she walked over and got on John's horse.

After John had mounted the horse Two Stars put her arms around his middle and laid her head on John's shoulder. Two Stars waited until they were almost home before she told John why Little Dove was really there.

"Talking Bear sent her to stay with me because you won't let Red Hawk do it." She said.

"You know that James thinks he's in love with her, don't you?" John asked without looking back.

Two Stars thought of what Little Dove had told her about her and

James and smiled.

"Do you think she feels the same about him?" John asked.

"Yes." Two Stars said as she looked back at them.

When the braves had returned to the village Snow Beaver went straight to Talking Bear.

"Where is Red Hawk?" Talking Bear asked when he saw that Red Hawk wasn't with them.

Just as Gray Wolf was about to speak Snow Beaver started telling Talking Bear everything. He told him how Red Hawk had found a white child and instead of killing her like he had been ordered he brought her back here. Every brave there could hear the anger in Talking Bear's voice as he spoke.

"If he hadn't followed my orders at the river then he must have taken the child to the slave girl."

The thought of Red Hawk not obeying orders left Talking Bear with a bad feeling.

"Do you want me to go get him?" Snow Beaver asked Talking Bear The thought of Snow Beaver going against Red Hawk brought a smile to Gray Wolf's face. Talking Bear turned to face Snow Beaver before he spoke.

"No, I think it would be best if we let Red Hawk come to us when he is ready he told him."

Emma had waited for Red Hawk at the creek and had stopped him as he reached her.

"I want to take you with me back to the village but Talking Bear has ordered me to stay away from you." Red Hawk told Emma.

"I couldn't go with you anyway I may be treated like a sister but I'm still a slave by law." Emma told him.

Emma could see how angry her words had made Red Hawk. "If you come and be my women no one will call you a slave again; you will be free of the whites forever." Red Hawk told Emma in a lower tone.

"I must go and report to Talking Bear about the little girl then I'll ask him if I can bring you into the village." He said as he got back on the horse.

"I will ask Master Adam how much he would have to have for you to buy me." Emma said as she watched Red Hawk ride off.

Emma waited until Red Hawk was out of sight before filling the water buckets and hurrying back to the cabin and Rose.

As Emma entered the cabin she found both Ruth and Liz chasing Rose around the cabin trying to take off her dirty dress. Rose had run into James's room and locked the door.

"What's the matter maw?" Emma asked as she sat down the buckets. "We is just trying to take off them dirty clothes and she ran in there." Liz said pointing at the door.

"You open this door right now Rose, you hear me?" Emma was saying through the door.

The tone of Emma's voice surprised Ruth and Liz at the same time. It sounded like a mother talking to her child. They were even more surprised when they heard the sound of the lock being removed. When the door opened Emma reached out her hand to Rose and smiled.

"Here I will help." Emma said as she led Rose to the wash basin.

Emma couldn't understand why when she tried to help Rose with her dress Rose pushed her hand away.

"No." Rose said when Emma reached for the dress again. Rose reached behind her and held the seam as tight as she could with her little hand.

"Now Rose we don't have time for this." Emma told her as she turned Rose around and unbuttoned the dress.

The smile that once belonged to Emma was lost when Emma discovered what Rose was hiding.

"No." Rose said as she turned her back away from them and cried. Both Emma and Liz had seen a black whipped like that but it was the first time they saw a white child like that. They could tell that it was just as much of a shock to Ruth as it was to them. Rose could see the tears in Emma's eyes as she knelt down and hugged the crying child. Emma had heard stories about white masters that treated their slaves like this but never their own child.

"Who did this to you child?" Ruth asked as she stood behind Emma.

"Was it your mother?" Ruth asked.

Rose looked up at Ruth and wiped the tears from her eyes and shook her head no.

"Who was it then?" Ruth asked in a confused voice.

"Pa." Rose said as she looked away.

After Emma wiped off her own tears then she turned Rose around and began taking off the dress.

"These are good people here Rose, no one will ever do this to you again." Emma told her.

Rose looked at Emma like she didn't believe her.

"Don't you get whopped?" Rose asked in a low voice so only Emma could hear her.

Emma looked at both Ruth and Liz before she answered Rose.

"No never like that Master Adam and Miss Ruth don't stand for anyone cutting up their slaves like that." Emma told her.

"Pa whipped his slaves worse than me when he had some."

"Your pa wasn't a very good man." Emma told Rose as she let the dirty dress hit the floor.

"You wouldn't believe what this child has been through." Ruth said as Adam and George came through the door.

James became confused when he asked John where he was going to sleep tonight and he said it depends. "Depends on what?" James asked even more confused by the way his brother was acting.

"It depends on where the bear skin is lying when we enter the cabin." John said then laughed.

"Maybe I should just go home." James was saying as John pushed his way through the door.

"Just let Little Dove decide." John was saying as he pushed on James.

Two Stars was letting Little Dove feel the baby move as the two came through the door. The two girls looked up just in time to see James's eyes go to the bear skin lying in the corner. James didn't understand the smile on everyone's faces but his. John walked over and put his arms around Two Stars and gently hugged her.

"You have been a bad girl today." He said laughingly.

"Maybe you should spank me." Two Stars told him.John's eyes went from James to Little Dove when James said something about going home again. Little Dove looked at Two Stars then walked over and stood by James.

"Please don't go." She said looking into James's eyes.

Little Dove couldn't help but laugh when she saw James's eyes go from her to the bear skin in the corner.

"It's going to be alright I guess." James said and began laughing along with John and Little Dove.

They all noticed that Two Stars wasn't laughing along with them so their laughter died too.

"Didn't you find that funny?" John asked thinking that Two Stars might have an objection to it.

"I can think of one person that wouldn't find it a bit funny." Two Stars said as she looked toward the village.

"Are you talking about Talking Bear?" Little Dove asked as she too lost her smile.

"It's the little girl you're talking about isn't it?" John asked.

"Red Hawk is in a lot of trouble isn't he?" Little Dove asked.

"What kind of trouble." John asked now just as fearful as the girls.

"It's the child Red Hawk brought here today. He had been ordered to kill anyone that was still alive." Two Stars told them.

"Red Hawk saw that the child didn't have the fever so he brought her here instead of killing her like he was ordered."

"But the little girl wasn't sick that stands for something doesn't it?" John asked.

Two Stars took her hand and felt the soft skin on his cheek before she spoke again.

"There's so much you need to know about the people of the village John. By not following Talking Bear's orders about the little girl he has put us all in danger she told him."

It came to John just then of how serious this thing was getting. "What will Talking Bear do to Red Hawk?" James asked as he looked at Little Dove.

"He could be run out of the village or killed." Little Dove said knowing the law as well as Two Stars.

All eyes were on Little Dove as she stared toward the village and wondered what waited for Red Hawk there.

"I don't see the problem." James said and got everyone's attention.

"Once maw and Emma gets the girl cleaned up and Talking Bear sees she isn't sick he will forget the whole thing won't he?" James asked.

John shook his head from side to side.

"No, no, James it means that when Red Hawk brought the girl here he put us in as much danger as he is in." John told him.

"Talking Bear has the right to have us all killed if he chooses to." Two Stars added.

"Do you really think that Talking Bear will go that far?" Little Dove asked.

"It's true the two of them grew up together but Talking Bear could not let Red Hawk get away with something like that for nothing. He would have to make Red Hawk an example for the rest of the braves."

"I can't believe that your brother Clay would treat a slave like that let alone his own child." Ruth said angrily.

Adam knew that there was no defiance for his little brother's actions and hung his head instead.

"I guess his drinking was even worse than I thought." Adam said when he did speak.

Liz was surprised to see George butting in on Master Adam who was talking with Miss Ruth.

"Master Adam, what's we going to do about that little girl in there?" George said pointing toward the room where Emma was giving Rose a bath.

"I was thinking Master Adam beings she gets along with Emma so well she should come and live with us." he said.

Liz was sure that what George was saying was going to bring them a lot of trouble but she said nothing. Ruth started to say something until she looked at the room where the two girls were.

"In order for Rose to be able to stay here she would be in James's room. And Master James won't let her stay in there." George smiled when Adam agreed to let Rose go live with them.

George thought by giving Emma someone to care for she would forget about the Indian boy. George thought if he didn't keep the two of them apart his baby would have a baby of her own. What George didn't know was if it was the idea of Emma having a baby or her having an Indian baby that scared him the most.

They all fell quiet at the door to James's room. Emma kept her eyes on Rose as she gently washed her. Emma thought of how on the trip here Rose would always come and walk with her. Back then Emma thought that it was because Rose just wanted a friend for the trip. As Emma looked at the lash marks on the girl's back Emma knew it was to get away from this. Emma reached and picked up the towel that she had laid down beside her.

"You tell me if this hurts ok." Emma said as she gently dried the child's back. Rose remembered how on the way out here she had always felt safe with Emma. She remembered also the times her pa had whipped her for walking with her.

"You are safe here, now Red Hawk and I will see to that." Emma told Rose as she dried her back.

Emma smiled as she handed Rose two dresses that Liz had made for her when she was a little girl.

"You can wear these until we can make you some more." Emma said as she handed Rose the dresses.

Rose turned around and hugged Emma then turned to the dirty

torn dress lying on the floor.

"My maw made that one." She said as she stared at the dress. "I will wash it and keep it for you." Emma said as she walked over and picked up the dress.

"Once I get it clean I'll let you keep it with my things." Emma told Rose as she came back to her.

Rose slipped one of the dresses over her head then smiled up at Emma.

With the morning chores done Emma and Rose were sitting under the big shade tree overlooking the creek.

"I think Master James has got a bed wench over at Master John's cabin." Emma told Rose as she stared toward the creek.

"Emma what is a bed wench?" Rose asked in a low voice.

Emma turned back to Rose and smiled before she answered her.

"It's a girlfriend." Emma told Rose who stared at her taking in every word she said.

"Is Master James's girlfriend an Indian?" Rose asked.

"Of course Rose, the only thing around here is Indians." Emma said as she looked toward the creek again.

"What are you looking for?" Rose asked.

"I thought I saw something." Emma said as she jumped to her feet and started toward the creek.

Emma started to say something to Rose when she too got to her feet and started following her. Emma knew that Rose did it because of her love.

"Who is it?" Rose asked when she reached where Emma was standing by the creek.

"I don't know yet." Emma said waiting with a longing to see Red Hawk again.

Rose had only seen James from a distance a couple of times and was eager to see him up close. Red Hawk seemed to just appear out of nowhere and Rose new him from the river.

"Him?" Rose asked as she pointed at Red Hawk.

"Yes." Emma said and started toward him.

Emma could tell that Red Hawk wasn't there just for fun when she saw his face.

"You and the child must come with me right now." Red Hawk said as he reached and grabbed Emma by the arm more roughly than she liked.

Rose stayed out of Red Hawk's reach but she didn't run.

"What are you talking about?" Emma asked with fear in her voice.

"Talking Bear is coming to kill everyone here and I'll take you to a safe place."

"You must trust me again." He told Rose.

Little Dove had enjoyed being with James for the last week. It was true that James had a lot of boyish ways about him but he loved her, that she was sure. He showed her his love with every glance. John had accepted them as a couple and Two Stars was the only one that seemed to object it. Both Two Stars and Little Dove stood in silence and watched as John and James rode toward Adam's cabin. As soon as the two boys were out of sight Little Dove let out a loud gasp. The sound made Two Stars turn toward her friend. She saw that Little Dove's face showed fear.

"What is it?" Two Stars asked Little Dove.

"I don't know but as soon as they got out of sight a cold feeling came over me." She said.

There was one thing that Two Stars had learned from growing up with Little Dove.

Pay close attention to her feelings. Now Two Stars could feel the cold hand of death as well.

George was helping Adam cut firewood for the winter when he noticed the girls gone from under the shade tree.

"Where you recon them girls went to Master Adam?" He asked as he looked toward the creek.

"Oh, they must have went to play in the water as hot as it is." Adam said as he wiped the sweat from his eyes.

"At least they were headed in that direction." Adam told George who stood staring at the creek bed.

"Go ahead George and check on them if you want." Adam said as he too headed for a shade tree himself.

"I'll do that Master Adam." George said as he started for the creek without looking at Adam.

Just as George reached the crest of the hill he saw Red Hawk ride off with both girls. George ran back to where Adam was resting.

"Master Adam that Indian has done stoled my Emma and the child." Gorge said in shock.

Adam could see the fear in George's face.

"Maybe he is just giving them a ride." He said.

Adam had told George that just to calm him down but Adam didn't believe it either.

"Get the horses ready George." Adam ordered over his shoulder as he headed for his cabin and his gun.

Adam didn't like the idea of taking the gun but his gut told him that he was going to need it before the day was over with.

When Red Hawk heard two riders coming toward him his first thoughts were that it was braves Talking Bear had sent after him. Before the riders came into view Red Hawk turned the horse deeper into the woods.

"Is your house this way" Rose asked as Red Hawk took the horse even deeper into the woods.

"No." Emma said from behind him.

"Now you quit asking so many questions." Emma said as she took her hand and tugged on Rose's dress.

"I am taking you to Two Stars, the only one who can save you." Red Hawk said then turned the horse toward the cabin and Two Stars.

Emma saw the cabin and smiled.

Adam rushed toward John as he and James entered the camp.

"Did you see Red Hawk and the girls?" He asked even before the horses were stopped.

"George said he thought they were headed toward your cabin." Adam said as he pointed behind John.

"No pa we didn't see anyone and if Red Hawk was going to my cabin we would have passed him."

"Then he must be taking them to the village." Adam was saying while shaking his head.

"Did you bring the guns?" Adam asked as George handed him the lead rains to the horse.

"Yes Master Adam." George said as he handed Adam the horse.

"Do you think you're going to need that?" John asked pointing at the gun. "Boy, it's better to have a gun and not need it than to need a gun and not have one." Adam said as he mounted the horse.

John caught up to Adam as fast as he could.

"I will ride ahead and tell Two Stars what is going on and get my gun as well." John said.

Adam shook his head in agreement as John road ahead of them.

"What's wrong?" Two Stars asked as she watched Little Dove staring out the door.

"I don't know it's just a feeling that I've had all day for something bad was coming. I feel danger for someone but I don't know what the danger is for." Little Dove said as she turned back toward Two Stars.

Both Two Stars and Little Dove heard the sound of footsteps on the porch. The last person Two Stars expected to ever come through that door was rushing in it.

"Red Hawk, what are you doing?" Two Stars asked as he came through the door pushing a child in front of him.

"Red Hawk, what are you doing with these girls?" Little Dove asked even before he could answer Two Starz's question.

All four girls stood staring at Red Hawk and waiting for him to say something.

"All that I know is that Talking Bear has ordered all the white camp to be burned." Red Hawk paused before he told them the rest.

"He has ordered that everyone to be killed." Red Hawk said as he turned back to Emma.

Both Two Stars and Little Dove's mouths flew open when they realized what Red Hawk meant.

"Why does Talking Bear want the whites dead?" Two Stars asked.

"He is going to attack the camp today." Red Hawk said as he turned his eyes back outside.

"Why did you bring them here Red Hawk, you know that Talking Bear will kill them here just as easy as at the white camp." Two Stars said.

Little Dove was just as puzzled as Two Stars to see a smile come to Red Hawk's face.

"Talking Bear can kill all the white's he wants to at the white camp but he can harm no one here."

"And why not?" Little Dove asked.

"Because this is a home of a tribal Chief and to spill blood on it would mean death." Red Hawk said and turned his eyes back outside.

"Even Talking Bear wouldn't break that law."

"If Talking Bear put the life of a future Chief in danger he would be run out of the village."

"What about my people?" Emma asked with fear in her voice.

"What about the rest of the white's?" Two Stars asked.

"If they try to fight against Talking Bear they will all be killed." Red Hawk said as he looked at Emma.

"You must go warn them little brother." Little Dove said as she stepped up beside Two Stars.

"There is no place they can go that Talking Bear can't get them." Red Hawk said as he looked outside again.

"Yes there is, bring them here." Two Stars said.

"There isn't enough room here for everyone." Red Hawk said.

"I can't believe that my little brother would not try and save the life of the boy that saved his and my life." Little Dove said.

Red Hawk could see that every eye in that cabin was on him. He knew that his sister was right and left.

"He did come here." John said to himself when he saw Red Hawk's horse standing by the porch.

"There's Master John." Emma said when she saw him getting off his horse.

"What's going on Red Hawk?" John asked angrily.

"Talking Bear has ordered that you all be killed so I brought them here to save their lives." Red Hawk said just as angrily.

Adam and the rest reached to where John and Red Hawk were talking just as Two Stars did.

"John you must go with him and get the rest of your people." Two Stars said as she pushed John toward his horse.

"Come on George, we are going as well." Adam said as he too got back onto his horse.

"James you stay here and watch the girls." John told him as they rode off.

"Get them back here as soon as you can and I'll explain everything!" Two Stars yelled as they rode away.

George wasn't sure what was going on but he knew that whatever it was it was bad. He followed behind them without a sound.

After Snow Beaver told Talking Bear that Red Hawk had left the village there was no doubt in Talking Bear's mind where he had gone. He was going to save the slave girl.

"We will take care of that tomorrow." Talking Bear said as he mounted his horse.

"Right now we will attack the whites at the camp." Talking Bear told Gray Wolf as they rode out of the village.

Gray Wolf was surprised to see Snow Beaver ride up to Talking Bear's right where Red Hawk always rode. Snow beaver smiled at Talking Bear like a child going to a playground instead of a war.

"He has no idea what is about to happen, does he?" Talking Bear asked as he turned to Gray Wolf.

"Do you want me to take some braves and get the white's at the boy's place?" Snow Beaver asked still wearing the smile.

Talking Bear stopped his horse and turned to Snow Beaver.

"Two Stars carries a future tribal Chief it will mean death for you to spill blood there."

"What does Adam think he is doing by going to that village?" Ruth was saying as she paced back and forth over the floor.

"I sure he stopped and got the boys to go with him." Ruth said more for her sake the Liz's.

"Miss Ruth, what them Indians going to do to my Emma?" Liz asked as she wiped her tears.

"Now Liz you don't be worrying yourself like that, you know them Indians has left us alone so far."

"The only reason they haven't is because of Master John being married to Miss Two Stars." Liz was saying as she wiped another tear.

"I believe that's the first time I ever heard you call Two Stars by her name." Ruth said as she sat down beside Liz.

The sound of fast moving horses brought both women to their feet.

"You two get on these horses." Adam ordered from the back of his horse.

"What about our things?" Ruth asked as she mounted the horse as ordered.

"Here Liz you get on this one." John told her in a commanding voice.

Little Dove stared at Emma to where she felt like she was on an auction block. Rose was just as much watching the Indian women as they were Emma. Rose stayed close to Emma's side but kept her eyes on Little Dove.

"I'm not going to hurt you." Little Dove said as she sat down beside Rose.

Little Dove took her finger and lifted the blond curls of Rose's hair. Two Stars laughed when Rose took Little Dove's long black hair and gave it a yank.

Emma gently smacked the back of Rose's hand and said "no."

"The child was only taking up for herself." Two Stars was saying after she stopped laughing.

Two Starz's face took on a serious look as she walked to the door and looked out again.

"Does you think they will get back soon?" Emma asked as she joined Two Stars at the door.

James stood watching the path as well, he was sure that they would have come back by now. As he turned around he saw Two Stars was too.

Adam had taken Ruth and Liz to the cabin while John and George gathered up all the powder and guns from the camp.

"Here comes pa and maw!" James yelled from his place by the path.

A smile came to Two Starz's face as she ran to the porch expecting to see John as well.

When the only people she saw were Adam, Ruth, and Liz she lost her smile.

"Come in!" Two Stars yelled to them from her place on the porch.

Red Hawk stood beside James and watched as John and George made it there without harm.

"Wait!" John yelled as Red Hawk turned to leave.

"Red Hawk I want to thank you for saving my family." John said as he got off his horse.

"We are even then." Red Hawk said as he turned to James.

John watched as Two Stars and Emma came toward them from the porch.

"If we live through this I'll set Emma free." John promised.

"She is not yours too set free." Red Hawk said.

George watched as Emma ran to Red Hawk and threw her arms

around him. When George looked at James and saw a smile on his face he understood Emma better.

"Here you might need this." John said as he handed Red Hawk one of the guns and powder.

All four men were surprised when Red Hawk pushed Emma away and stepped back from them.

"I will not let you spill blood on this ground either." Red Hawk said angrily pointing at the ground.

Seeing that John still didn't understand why they were safe here and not at the camp. Red Hawk placed a hand on John's shoulder before he spoke.

"The baby that Two Stars carries could be a boy child and a future Chief."

"If Talking Bear ever spilt blood on the sacred ground of a Chief he would die for it. If Two Stars had already had had the child and it was a girl we all would be dead by now. You should hope that your child is a boy." He said.

Two Stars watched as everyone but Red Hawk came through the door and just stood there.

"You can sit there." She said pointing at the floor.

Before he sat down James walked over and picked up the bear skin for them to sit on. All eyes looked at John as a smile came to his face. All of them wondered just what he found funny about this but said nothing. John quickly lost his smile when he saw everyone looking at him.

"Do you think they will come today?" Rose asked looking at Two Stars.

"If Talking Bear said today he will be here today." She told everyone now looking at her.

"My brother isn't in the habit of risking his life for a lie." Little Dove said angrily.

"You see to our people the lowest form of people are the ones that will tell a lie." Two Stars said.

"I meant no harm, I'm sorry." Ruth told Little Dove not knowing her name.

All eyes went to Emma standing by the door when she said, "Their here."

Red Hawk stood staring at Gray Wolf and Talking Bear as they rode up to him.

"Where are the white's from the camp?!" Talking Bear yelled and pointed toward the Huff camp.

There was no doubt to Red Hawk that they had been to the camp and found no one. Just as Red Hawk was about to speak Two Stars and Little Dove stepped out onto the porch.

"What have they done my brother that you bring warriors to my door?" Two Stars asked to see if he would lie to her.

Talking Bear looked over his shoulder at the braves behind him before he spoke.

"The child is sick and brings death to our people and I'm here to see that don't happen."

"Brother, you know that the child is not sick and you want her dead." Two Stars was saying as she came off the porch and straight to Talking Bear.

"This is the home of a Chief you will not harm anyone here." She said looking at the braves behind Talking Bear.

"These people are my blood now." Two Stars said patting her big belly.

"Everyone here is under my protection do you understand?" She said this time looking at Talking Bear.

Snow Beaver came up beside Talking Bear then asked, "Is Red Hawk under your protection too?"

"I need no one's protection from you Snow Beaver if you care to pick a spot in the village I will race you there." Red Hawk said as he walked up to Snow Beaver's horse.

As Red Hawk looked at Gray Wolf he thought he saw him smile.

"Or you want to be remembered as the Chief that spilt blood on the ground of a chief?" Two Stars asked.

While she talked, Talking Bear turned to look at the braves behind him.

"I will keep these people here if I must and see that they do not come to the village." She said.

"If just one of you gets sick I will kill you all sister."

Talking Bear Turned his attention to Red Hawk.

"You and Little Dove cannot return to the village either!" Talking Bear yelled down at Red Hawk.

"Where are we to go?" Little Dove asked.

"To me you two are no better than the whites so see if they will let you stay with them."

"And if no one comes down with the sickness?" Red Hawk asked.

Talking Bear didn't say a word as he turned his horse and left.

Red Hawk turned to Little Dove as Talking Bear left and said "Sorry."

"You can stay here as long as you like." Two Stars said as she put an arm around Little Dove.

"That means you to Red Hawk." She told him as he turned toward the village.

"Only Gold Eagle of the village council can keep us from the village forever." Red Hawk said.

"He may be able to protect us at the village but he has no power over Talking Bear outside the village." Little Dove said.

The sound of the front door coming open brought every one's attention to it. James and Emma came out and looked at them. They had all waited until all of the braves had left before they came out onto the porch.

"What did Talking Bear say he was going to do?" Adam asked when he reached Two Stars.

Even before Two Stars could answer Adam's first question he asked another one.

"What is he going to do about our cabins?" He asked.

"I would say that you will have to rebuild." Two Stars said as she watched the black smoke climb into the sky to mingle with the white clouds.

"Oh look." Ruth said as her and Liz joined the others in watching the smoke.

"Where are we going to live now?" Ruth asked as she put her arms around Adam and cried.

"We all can't stay here and now we can't go back there." Adam said pointing toward what was their home.

"Do you think Talking Bear will let them build the cabins again?" John asked as he turned to Two Stars.

"He will have to if I live there too." Two Stars said then turned and went back inside.

Rose stood and watched as the grownups talked back and forth to one another. It reminded her of how the people at the river acted when the sickness came. Her mother took her to the cave and kept her there just before the Indian's killed everyone.

"Is it going to happen to me again?" She asked herself as she watched them.

Adam turned to John and looked past him toward the cabin.

"We all can't stay in the cabin so we men will stay out here and let the women have the cabin." He said.

"That sounds good to me." Little Dove said as she headed for the cabin.

"I'll go and get the things we'll need for the night." James told Adam and followed Little Dove to the cabin.

"That boy sure is acting strange." Adam said as he watched James walk away. "Everything he does at his age seems strange pa." John said then laughed. Red Hawk didn't find John's words funny at all. It was at that moment that Red Hawk understood where Talking Bear's fear of the white's came from because Red Hawk felt it to. Red Hawk now saw the whites as a beast that destroyed anything in front of them. Now the only Chief that he served had the blood of that beast in him Red Hawk thought. Village law was the safety of a living chief it said nothing about his blood, he told himself. He stood watch for trouble while the others fixed the camp for the night.

Gray Wolf and Snow Beaver had been sent to keep watch on the whites. They both sat as quiet as they could not more than one hundred feet from the busy men.

"One of us must go and tell Talking Bear what the whites are doing." Snow Beaver said to Gray Wolf.

"I couldn't leave you here alone with these people so you go and I'll stay here." Gray Wolf told him.

Snow Beaver thought he had just been insulted but he was going to get to go talk to the Chief. Maybe I'll get Gray Wolf next he thought. If Talking Bear would give him a few braves he could sneak in their camp and kill them in their sleep. Something like that would put him in his rightful place right beside Talking Bear. Snow Beaver rode straight to Talking Bear's teepee. He found the Chief pacing back and forth waiting for the report. Talking Bear liked Snow Beaver's loyalty but he never used his head for anything except a place to carry his feathers. Talking Bear could tell what most of his braves were thinking by just a look. But with Gray Wolf it was different he could look at him all day and not tell what he thought. His thinking brought Talking Bear's thoughts back to Red Hawk and his betrayal to him. Gray Wolf was a good brave and a brave he could trust to fill Red Hawk's place. Talking Bear was surprised to see Snow Beaver bringing the report instead of Gray Wolf.

"Well what is it?" Talking Bear asked as he sat down.

Both Two Stars and Little Dove burst out laughing as James reached and picked up the bear skin from the floor. Ruth and Liz looked at each other and wondered what those two were laughing at. Both Emma and Rose joined in the laughing and had no idea what they were laughing at.

"What?" James asked as he stared at the laughing girls.

"Oh nothing just be careful who you share that with." Little Dove said pointing at the bear skin James was holding.

"For your sake don't hand it to Red Hawk." Two Stars told him while holding back her laughter.

James shook his head and without a word walked out.

John turned to Red Hawk who was down on his face as he watched James come toward them.

"What's wrong with that Indian?" George asked.

"He's praying George, he is praying." John said.

"What's he praying for Master John?" George asked.

"He is praying that no one can see his face right now." John said then laughed.

Talking Bear sat smoking his pipe when Snow Beaver entered his teepee.

"Talking Bear we have them just where we want them." He said as he sat down by Talking Bear.

"The men are making camp outside and the women are safe inside." Snow Beaver said excitedly.

"I want to take a few braves and kill the white men tonight." He said with the same excitement.

Talking Bear got to his feet and threw the pipe he was holding to the ground.

"The whole village knows by now that Two Stars is carrying a baby. The child could someday become a tribal Chief and you want to spill blood at his door?!" Talking Bear yelled angrily.

"Your only job is to watch them nothing more, do you understand?"

"Now go do as you're told." Talking Bear said as he pointed toward the door. Gray Wolf rose to his feet when Snow Beaver returned to him.

"What did Talking Bear say?" Gray Wolf asked.

When Rose opened her eyes she was face to face with a sleeping Emma. Once she got to her feet she could tell that the rest were asleep as well. Rose could see her own breath in the early morning air and knew the sun had just come up. As quietly as she could Rose made her way to the door and opened it. As she stepped out onto the porch it took her eyes a few seconds to adjust to the light. Once her eyes had adjusted to the light she strained them looking for Red Hawk. She saw that he wasn't sleeping with the other men; he must be gone by now she thought as she stepped off the porch in her quest to find him.

"What are you doing out here?" He asked as he turned Rose around to face him.

"They is all asleep." Rose said pointing at the cabin.

"It's the same here." Red Hawk told Rose as they looked at the sleeping men. "You must go back in the cabin and stay." He said.

Rose shook her head no but her feet carried her toward the cabin door.

Little Dove was standing by the door as Rose came back into the cabin.

"Did my brother frighten you?" She asked as Rose stood and stared at her. Without a word Rose shook her head no to Little Dove's question.

"Is something wrong?" Two Stars asked as she joined Little Dove at the door. "What's the matter Rose?" Emma asked while using the back of her hand to rub her eyes.

Rose quickly walked to where Emma stood and got behind her. "I think she is afraid of us." Little Dove told Two Stars as she held out her hand to Rose.

"Can you blame her after watching Indians kill everyone she knew?" Ruth said as she and Liz joined them.

Little Dove could see the anger flash in Two Starz's eyes and knew she was about to tell Ruth just what she was thinking.

"Can I speak to you on the porch?" Little Dove said as she pushed Two Stars out the door.

"Them Indians is what saved us isn't it?" Liz asked.

Ruth walked to where she could see the men as they began to wake from their sleep. She watched as Two Stars and Little Dove started toward the men. James and George were laying side by side on the bear skin sound asleep. James rolled over and his arm landed across George's shoulder making it look like he was giving George a hug. John couldn't help but laugh out loud and when Two Stars and Little Dove saw what John was laughing at they started laughing too. James's eyes came open from their laughing and the way George jumped to his feet and stared at him. Two Stars and Little dove stopped laughing when they saw that Ruth and Liz had started the morning fire. The white smoke had to fight its way through the morning mist to reach the cloud now.

"They just don't understand our ways." Little Dove told her as Two Stars watched the cabin.

"Is something wrong?" John asked.

Adam found the camp just as he had expected. Burned to the ground. Two Stars had come with them to see what Talking Bear had done and to keep the whites safe.

"There isn't anything left Master Adam." George said as he stood looking at the burned cabins.

"You know George you are wrong." Adam told him as he looked at all the dead trees lying before him.

"What are you talking about pa?" John asked as he came up beside George.

Adam didn't answer John he just went on with his counting of the trees. John saw a smile come to Adam's face as he got down off his horse and walked away from them. George walked over to where Adam stood.

"Master Adam does you want me to start making logs ready for a cabin?" He asked.

"No George, first we build a wall around this place then we build the cabins." Adam said as he turned to Two Stars.

"The next time Talking Bear calls on us he is going to find Fort Huff in his way."

John could tell by the expression on Two Starz's face that her heart was being pulled in two different directions at the same time. Adam had instructed everyone to dig a ditch to place the poles in once they were cut.

"How deep do you think pa wants this ditch?" James asked as he sank the pick back into the ground.

"I don't know just keep digging until he tells you to stop." John told him.

Red Hawk took his place under a tree as the whites dug a little hole in the ground. He had no idea what they were doing but he was sure Talking Bear wasn't going to like it at all.

Red Hawk was surprised when Two Stars told them, "If they built her and John a cabin there that Talking Bear couldn't harm them again."

"I'm here to protect the little Chief and nothing more." Red Hawk told himself as he sat down.

As soon as he had taken his seat Red Hawk saw George headed toward him carrying two picks in his hands. Red Hawk gave George a look that told him no. Red Hawk saw the anger in Emma's face as she took the pick from her pa and headed for the ditch. Two Stars walked over to where Red Hawk was and stood staring at him.

"Red Hawk, remember when you told me you couldn't stand the way the whites treated their slaves?" Two Stars asked.

Red Hawk waited a few seconds before he shook his head yes.

"Do you call what you did to Emma any better?" She asked as she looked at Emma digging the ditch.

"If you love her like you say you do then go show her." Two Stars said just before she turned and left.

Rose walked up to Emma and tugged at her arm when she saw Red Hawk coming their way. It was at that moment that Emma knew that Red Hawk really loved her and she would be his and free forever.

"You go stay over there with the child." Red Hawk said pointing toward Rose.

Without a word Emma kissed him then left.

The night before Snow Beaver had stayed at the village while Gray Wolf watched the whites. It was early morning so Snow Beaver quietly made his way to where Gray Wolf was supposed to be watching the cabin. Snow Beaver didn't find Gray Wolf there but what was even stranger than that he could not see the whites either.

"I must get back to the village and tell Talking Bear what I found or didn't find here."

It was after he got back to his horse and started toward the village when he saw all the horse tracks going toward the burned out camp. Just as Snow Beaver reached the creek bed Gray Wolf stepped out in front of him to stop him.

"You won't believe what they are doing over there." Gray Wolf said pointing toward the camp.

"They brought Two Stars and Red Hawk with them and now Red Hawk is digging in the ground like a white man." Gray Wolf told him.

"When is Talking Bear coming?" Gray Wolf asked looking back down the trail that Snow Beaver had just come down.

"I can't believe Talking Bear let Red Hawk be in charge of the braves all this time." Snow Beaver said as Gray Wolf lied down beside him.

"Just look at him digging in the ground like a ground hog." Snow Beaver said then laughed.

"He would be easy to hit from here." Snow Beaver said as he turned to Gray Wolf.

"We have no orders to kill anyone." Gray Wolf said angrily.

"Lucky for you Red Hawk, today I will just take your job instead of your life." Snow Beaver said louder than he wanted.

"What?" Gray Wolf asked not sure he had heard Snow Beaver right.

"Oh nothing I was just thinking out loud." Snow Beaver said not even looking at Gray Wolf.

Gray Wolf had known Snow Beaver his whole life and he never knew him to think out load or any other way for that matter.

Gray Wolf got to his feet and shook his head as he looked down at Snow Beaver. Without a word Gray Wolf made his way back to the horses. Snow Beaver was watching Red Hawk so close that he didn't notice that Gray Wolf had gone.

"Would you look at that?" Snow Beaver would say each time the pick sank into the ground.

When Red Hawk saw movement in the bushes he quickly dropped the pick and headed for the shade tree and his gun. Red Hawk sat down very quickly and didn't move. He knew that they were being watched but he didn't know by how many. As Snow Beaver turned his head to say something to Gray Wolf who wasn't there, Red Hawk was able to disappear into the trees. Snow Beaver could feel the hair stand on end when he couldn't see Red Hawk anywhere.

Both Two Stars and Little Dove saw Red Hawk as he vanished into the trees. Little Dove started to rise up for a better look when Two Stars placed a hand on her shoulder to stop her.

"Don't act like there is anything different." She said as she took back her hand.

Emma rose to her feet and walked over to where Red Hawk had dropped the pick before he left.

Rose watched Emma start digging before she walked over and stood right in front of Two Stars and Little Dove.

"Emma can't find him either." Rose said while pointing to where Red Hawk had disappeared into the trees.

Little Dove gently placed a hand on Rose's arm and pulled it down. John looked at James as he went about his work as if there wasn't something wrong. It appeared that the only ones that didn't see Red Hawk leave were James and Snow Beaver.

Adam and George turned to see John going about his work as usual so they did the same. Two Stars was glad to see that Rose had lost the fear of her and Rose gave her a missing tooth smile. Red Hawk found where Snow Beaver had tied his horse then made his way up behind Snow Beaver. A sound of a horse running behind Snow Beaver made him look behind him. He found Red Hawk standing over him with a gun just an inch from his head.

"Wait Red Hawk I'm just here to watch nothing more." Snow Beaver said as he got to his feet.

"If I didn't already know that you would be dead by now." Red Hawk said as he lowered the gun.

"It's time you went and made your report isn't it?" Red Hawk said pointing toward Snow Beaver.

"Oh by the way I think your horse got tired of waiting and left without you."

Red Hawk saw the anger flash in Snow Beaver's eyes as he reached for his knife. Red Hawk simply raised the gun and pulled back the hammer once again.

"You can tell Talking Bear one thing for me when you get back. Next time don't send a boy to do a man's job." Red Hawk said then smiled.

"Leave the arrows." Red Hawk ordered as Snow Beaver reached for his bow.

Red Hawk knew for a warrior to lose his arrows it was a shame to the village.

Emma took the back of her hand and wiped the sweat from her eyes. Her eyes started to burn from the salt that was mixed into her sweat. Once she got her sight back she saw Master Adam staring at the trees. She watched as he turned his eyes toward the sun then back to John.

"Them Indians would be expecting us to take a break about now." He said as he headed for the shade tree.

"No one had to be told twice as they all stopped what they were doing and headed for the shade."

James kept his eyes on Little Dove as he dropped the rock he was holding and almost hit his own foot as it fell to the ground. Emma was the last to head for the coolness of the shade and cool drink of water. Both Two Stars and Little Dove noticed how Rose took on the appearance of a frightened animal as she watched James coming her way. They watched as Rose jumped to her feet and quickly moved away as James reached them. Little Dove noticed that even though Rose had moved away from her she never took her eyes off James as he approached.

"Rose you don't have to be afraid of him." Little Dove said pointing at James.

Everyone noticed when Red Hawk came into the open and headed toward them. Two stars watched as Rose lost her frightened animal look and started to smile.

"Why is Rose so afraid of you?" Little Dove asked as James sat down beside her.

"I have no idea why she is afraid of me she has been like that since I first met her." James said as he sat down.

"Do you know why Emma?" James asked as he turned to her. "No Master James she never say anything to me about you." Emma said not looking at James but at Rose as she watched Red Hawk coming her way.

"The next time you talk to her you try and find out for me." James told Emma.

"Yes Master James I'll do that." Emma told him.

Snow Beaver was almost back to the village when he saw Talking Bear and fifty braves coming toward him.

"When Gray Wolf told me he left you there by yourself I thought Red Hawk had killed you by now." Talking Bear said as he stopped his horse.

"Where is your horse and arrows?" Talking Bear asked looking down at Snow Beaver.

"Red Hawk run my horse off and took my arrows away from me." Snow Beaver said looking at the ground instead of Talking Bear.

Gray Wolf didn't say anything but when Snow Beaver looked at him he saw him smile.

"Are we going to kill the whites and Red Hawk?" Snow Beaver asked as he looked at the fifty braves behind Talking Bear.

"Why do you want to kill Red Hawk after he let you live?" Talking Bear asked as he looked at him.

"As long as Two Stars is with the whites there is nothing I can do." Talking Bear said as he turned his horse around and headed back to the village.

"What about a ride?" Snow Beaver asked as all the braves turned and followed Talking Bear.

Gray Wolf stopped his horse and told Snow Beaver to think about his horse and arrows on his walk back to the village. Gray Wolf saw the anger flash in Snow Beaver's eyes just as he rode off to get back at Talking Bear's right side. As Snow Beaver watched the braves ride off he looked at the empty quiver of arrows and knew that it wasn't going to be any different back at the village. Snow Beaver wasn't as mad at the Braves that wouldn't give him a ride as he was at Red Hawk who had brought this shame on him.

"Red Hawk will pay for this." Snow Beaver said in a low voice as he watched the last brave vanish from sight.

Snow Beaver turned around to where he was facing the whites' camp and shook his fist in the air.

"Red Hawk I will take your heart as it beats in your chest." Snow Beaver said as he walked.

As his feet walked forward his eyes kept watch behind him just in case.

Two Stars and Little Dove's eyes looked at each other when they saw Red Hawk carrying a hand full of arrows without a quiver.

"What did you find out?" Adam asked out loud as he and George reached Red Hawk.

"Just a young brave doing what I used to do." Red Hawk said as he tossed the arrows on the ground.

Little Dove couldn't stop herself from smiling as the arrows landed at Adam's feet.

"There is no one there now." He said as he turned to Two Stars.

"The brave you took those from will hate you for not killing him." Two Stars told him as she pointed at the arrows and smiled.

"Snow Beaver would like to use those on me anyway." Red Hawk told her and smiled back.

Both Emma and rose followed Red Hawk to his shade tree and sat down with him. George thought that Master Adam would put the girl in her place but he said nothing to her. As George watched Emma siting and talking to Red Hawk he noticed her laughter of freedom.

"You might not like it but there is nothing we can do about it George." Adam said as he watched Emma and Red Hawk.

"When I brought all of us here I had no idea that things would turn out like they did." Adam said as he got to his feet.

He looked at John and James as they sat with the girls. "Then you is going to set my Emma free?" George asked as he too got to his feet.

"What would she do with freedom out here?" Adam asked as he headed back to work.

"Besides if it wasn't for these Indians we all would have died at the river with the others." Adam said over his shoulder as he walked.

Both John and James saw Adam heading back to the ditch and rose to their feet as well. Red Hawk decided that he could best be used by keeping watch instead of digging in the ground.

He made no move toward going back to work on that hole in the ground. Emma was surprised that Master Adam hadn't said something to her about what she was doing.

Gray Wolf followed Talking Bear into the teepee before he asked him any questions.

"Should I go keep watch on Red Hawk and the whites?" Gray Wolf asked.

Gray Wolf thought he had made a big mistake when Talking Bear turned to him in anger.

"Are you like Snow Beaver and want to kill Red Hawk and the whites too?" He asked angrily.

"No I have no need in seeing Red Hawk dead; I think he deserves my respect." Gray Wolf said loudly.

"As for the whites they matter not to me." He said in a lower voice. Talking Bear looked at Gray Wolf in silence for some time before he spoke again.

"You Gray Wolf will be my lead brave from now on." Talking Bear said as he stared out the door.

"It's obvious that Snow Beaver can't do the job." Talking Bear said more to himself than to Gray Wolf.

"If Two Stars has a boy it could someday become tribal Chief and I will not let that happen."

Talk Bear watched for Gray Wolf's reaction. Gray Wolf stood showing no reaction to Talking Bear's words so he went on.

"Two Starz's baby will not be of our blood and I will not let that happen to the village."

"What is it you want me to do?" Gray Wolf asked not sure what was expected of him.

"Right now nothing because the baby could be a girl and that would take care of the problem."

"You just keep a close watch and nothing else is that clear?" Talking Bear asked.

"As for Red Hawk you best leave him alone too or he may take your arrows too." Talking Bear said with a smile.

"You know that Snow Beaver was lucky that Red Hawk just took his arrows instead of his life." Talking Bear said staring back out the door.

"What are you going to do about the little girl?" Gray Wolf asked. "Everyone knows that the girl isn't sick with the fever or Two Stars wouldn't have her around the baby."

"For now leave them all alone." Talking Bear said as he motioned for Gray Wolf to leave him.

Red Hawk watched as Rose looked at him like he was a strange animal and it made him uneasy. The sound of Emma's laughing brought his attention back to her.

"She like's you is the reason she looks at you that way." Emma said then finished laughing.

"She makes me feel like an animal and I don't like it." Red Hawk told Emma as he turned back to Rose.

Emma stopped laughing and said, "Now you know how I have felt my whole life."

"What was he to become now that he had taken the slave girl for his mate? Was he freeing her or was she turning him into a red slave?" Red Hawk asked himself.

When Emma reached out to take Red Hawk by the hand he jerked his hand back very fast.

"I'm sorry." Emma said as she started to get to her feet.

"Me and Rose won't bother you again." Emma said once she was on her feet.

"Wait it's not what you think." Red Hawk said as he took Emma by the hand making her stop.

After Red Hawk made sure no one was looking he pulled Emma back down to his side.

"In the village a maiden and a brave cannot even touch hands until they are mates." Red Hawk told her as she sat beside him.

Little Dove sat talking to James about why Rose was so frightened of him so she didn't see her brother holding Emma's hand. As soon as Two Stars saw it she tapped Little Dove on the shoulder and pointed it out. Both women busted out in laughter. John couldn't understand what was so funny about Red Hawk holding Emma's hand. Two Stars saw the confusion on John's face and took his hand in hers before she spoke.

"You see John in village law it is not permitted for a brave and maiden to show affection in public."

Just as John was about to ask another question Little Dove joined the conversation.

"It is to insure that the maiden stays a maiden." She said with a laugh at the end.

"Does it work?" James asked in a serious voice.

Two Stars looked at Little Dove for a moment. Red Hawk was watching them laugh and quickly let go of Emma's hand. Just as he got to his feet Adam called out that it was time to go back to the cabin. James and Little Dove walked behind Emma and Red Hawk while Rose walked in front all the way back. Red Hawk could feel their eyes on him with every step he took. As soon as they had reached the safety of the cabin Red Hawk turned to face James.

"What is it you want?" He asked loudly.

"I want to give you my sister for yours." James said pointing at Emma.

"What about maw, pa, and Master Adam?" Emma asked in a frightened voice.

"What do you want to do Emma?" John asked once he and Two Stars joined the conversation.

Emma's thoughts were going in all different direction at the same time. Without a word she walked over and took Red Hawk by the hand for her answer.

"You know you can't take her back to the village."

Red Hawk suddenly got the feeling that he had just married into the white man's world.

He looked at Emma as she tried to get Rose to come and join them then toward the village.

Rose saw Emma coming toward her and calling her name. Instead of going to Emma Rose was backing away from her. As long as James was close to Emma Rose wasn't going to be her friend.

It was true that James hadn't done anything to her but the way he looked just like her pa frightened her. She had watched how her pa went from a loving pa to an evil man in seconds. To Rose if he looked like him that much he must be that much like him. Rose could feel the tears start to come to her eyes so she took her arm and wiped them.

"What's wrong Rose?" Emma asked as she approached her.

Rose couldn't find the words so she just shook her head no over and over.

"Red Hawk it is me also that can't go back to the village." Little Dove said as she turned to James.

"You and Little Dove can build your teepees here if you want." Two Stars told them.

"I will go tell pa and George if you want me to." John said then waited for Red Hawk's answer.

Red Hawk walked up to Emma and took her by the hand and shook his head yes.

"And I'll go with him." James said as he pointed for John to lead the way.

Just as the two boys was about to enter the cabin they noticed Emma walk away from Red Hawk.

"Wait." John said as he watched her coming toward them.

"We will let Emma go in first." John told James as he took hold of his arm.

Emma's heart was pounding so hard that she could hear it as she stepped through the door. Adam watched as the three of them came in one at a time. He started to say something to them until the three walked over to George.

"I know that my pa owns her but Red Hawk has asked for her hand and James and I think its ok with us." John said as he stopped in front of George.

"Master John we'z loves Emma with all our heart and would let her go but Master Adam is who will say if she is free to go Master John."

All eyes turned toward Adam as George talked. Adam rose to his feet and walked over and pulled open a box of papers.

"These are the titles to every slave I have ever owned." He said as he tossed them into the cook fire.

"Does that mean I'ez can go with Red Hawk?" Emma asked as she watched the papers burn.

"Yes Emma, that means that you are free." John said with a smile.

George and Liz looked at each other as the feeling of freedom surged through them. Ruth couldn't see what was so different from now and the time before the papers burned.

"Useless." She said to herself in a low voice.

Gray Wolf was just about to put his horse into the corral when Snow Beaver came up behind him.

"You have turned Talking Bear against me." Snow Beaver was saying as he stopped in front of Gray Wolf.

"You are the one that turned Talking Bear against you; I had nothing to do with it." Gray Wolf said angrily.

"It wasn't me who lost his arrows." Gray Wolf said then smiled.

Snow Beaver's hand went toward his knife very slowly. His hand came to a stop when Gray Wolf asked him a simple question.

"Do you really think you could win a knife fight with me?" He asked.

Gray Wolf's hand went to his knife just in case Snow Beaver was dumb enough to try. Gray Wolf watched as the anger shot through Snow Beaver's eyes from his words. He went on to say that Snow Beaver didn't have the brains he had thought if he tried. The anger still showed as Snow Beaver turned and walked away.

"If you can get your arrows back from Red Hawk you just might get back on Talking Bear's side." Gray Wolf said then laughed as Snow Beaver walked away.

The smile left Gray Wolf's face as he watched Snow Beaver get on his horse and ride toward Two Starz's cabin. Gray Wolf thought of when Talking Bear had told him to keep his eyes on Snow Beaver.

"Sorry old boy." He said to the horse as he got back on him and started after Snow Beaver.

Snow Beaver was already off his horse and hid in the bushes by the time Gray Wolf reached him.

"Just watch him was what Talking Bear had said to do." Gray Wolf told himself as he stopped behind Snow Beaver.

Snow Beaver was so interested in what was going on in front of him that he didn't even know that Gray Wolf was anywhere around. He looked to see where Red Hawk could be. Snow Beaver first saw movement under a large tree to his right and looked to see just what it was that made it.

There he was sitting with the child and the slave girl. The slave girl was telling Red Hawk something then she began to laugh. The sight of Red Hawk with a smile on his face brought back the hate Snow Beaver held for Red Hawk 10 fold. Snow Beaver had convinced himself that if he could kill the little girl that Talking Bear would take him back into the tribe. He was sure that as long as the girl was around Red Hawk he couldn't get to her.

"How am I going to get the girl away from Red Hawk and him not know it?" Snow Beaver had just asked himself when both girls rose to their feet.

It was as if the Great Spirit had approved his plan when they started walking away from Red Hawk. Snow Beaver saw what she headed for. The two girls were headed for a small out building that George had made for a toilet. Snow Beaver waited until the two girls had gone inside before he came up behind them.

"I will wait until they come out then kill the little girl with my knife." He told himself.

Snow Beaver's heart was pounding in his chest as he watched the outhouse door come open.

Rose waited and followed Emma out the door just in time to see Emma being hit in the head.

The sight of Emma being stabbed in the head by an Indian she had never seen before put Rose into shock. First it was fear that robbed Rose of sound but the next time it was because of Snow Beaver's hand stopped her. Just as Snow Beaver was about to plunge his knife into Rose he saw Red Hawk coming his way. A smile crossed Snow Beaver's face when he saw that Red Hawk was without his gun. Red Hawk saw Snow Beaver about the same time Snow Beaver saw him. By the time Red Hawk saw him Snow Beaver had pushed Rose to the ground and was putting his arrow into the bow. The sight of Snow Beaver pulling the bow string tight wasn't what frightened Red Hawk. That was when he saw Gray Wolf standing behind Snow Beaver with his bow already drawn. As soon as Gray Wolf let the arrow go Red Hawk just waited for it to hit its mark, Him. But to Red Hawk's surprise the arrow struck Snow Beaver in the back killing him instantly. Red Hawk waited to see if Gray Wolf was going to put another arrow into his bow for him. He was relieved when he saw Gray Wolf lower the bow and without a word walk away.

The sight of Emma and Snow Beaver lying on the ground brought Rose back her sound as she began to scream loudly. Rose stepped over the Indian with an arrow in his back and knelt beside Emma's lifeless body. Rose began to cry and shake all over.

"Who can I trust now Emma?" Rose asked.

Red Hawk thought that Emma was dead when he saw her lying on the ground. From out of nowhere Little Dove dropped to her knees beside Emma. Red Hawk watched as his sister checked Emma's vital signs for life.

"She's still alive." Little Dove told him.

"We must get her inside." Little Dove said as she looked at Red Hawk.

He picked Emma up in his arms and ran for the cabin.

"Come on Rose and I'll take you to her." Two Stars said as she reached out her hand to her.

Adam, George, and the boys were loading their guns as Red Hawk came through the door carrying Emma in his arms.

"Put her on the bed." Little Dove ordered as she followed Red Hawk through the door.

They all watched in silence as Red Hawk laid Emma on the bed as gently as he could.

"Is she dead?" Adam asked"

"Who killed her?" George asked as he stepped up to Red Hawk.

"She's not dead yet." Little Dove said as she sat on the bed beside Emma.

"Who did that to her?" Adam asked angrily.

"It was a brave called Snow Beaver." Red Hawk told George as he faced him. "I'll kill him." John said as he headed for the door.

"He is already dead he is lying out there by the small house." Red Hawk said.

"That'll show them Red Hawk." James said with a little laugh at the end.

"Think you Master Red Hawk for killing that Indian." George said holding out his hand to Red Hawk.

Red Hawk never made any attempt to take hold of George's hand.

"I was not the one who killed him it was a young brave by the name of Gray Wolf." Red Hawk said looking at Little Dove as he talked.

"Why did he want to hurt my Emma; she never done him no harm?" George asked.

"He wasn't after Emma he was after me; Emma just got in the way." Red Hawk said as he looked at her.

"Is that why Gray Wolf killed him?" Little Dove asked.

"No he did that to show me that Talking Bear had not ordered it." Red Hawk said.

"We should think Gray Wolf for his help." Adam told the gathering of men.

"Gray Wolf wasn't helping us he was simply doing his job as Talking Bear's right hand would do."

Red Hawk couldn't understand why these whites did not see the difference that Gray Wolf was Talking Bear's right hand made. Gray Wolf was young and wise for a brave and Red Hawk knew to respect him.

"Do you think Talking Bear will leave us alone now?" Adam asked hopefully.

"The only thing that it shows is that Snow Beaver went against the people of the village and paid for it with his life." Red Hawk told them.

The grownups were so engrossed in their talk that they never saw Rose get on her knees beside Emma's bed beginning to cry.

"Don't you die on me Emma you hear me." Rose was saying as she laid her head on Emma's bed.

"You are all I got." Rose was saying as she brushed away her tears.

"She will not die." Little Dove said as she led her away.

Gray Wolf wasn't sure what Talking Bear was going to do about him killing Snow Beaver to save Red Hawk's life. This had been his first mission as the Chief's number one brave and now it was more than likely his last. Like most of the people in the village Gray Wolf grew up in the belief that the lowest form of life was a liar. To Gray Wolf it would be better to die than to be called a liar by the whole village. He was going to tell Talking Bear the truth and accept whatever the Chief done to him. The old women were busy building their fires for the night as he rode into the village.

"I hope this time that it's for the rest of the night." He told the horse as he put him away for the second time that day.

The smile left Talking Bear's face as he saw the look on Gray Wolf's face. "Has something happened to Two Stars?" Talking Bear asked as he jumped to his feet.

"No, Two Stars is alright Talking Bear but Snow Beaver is dead." Gray Wolf said as they both sat back down.

"Leave us." Talking Bear ordered the other braves as Gray Wolf sat down.

"How did Red Hawk kill him?" Talking Bear asked once the other braves had left.

"Red Hawk didn't kill Snow Beaver; I was the one who killed him." Gray Wolf said.

"I killed him before he could spill blood on holy ground."

"He was going to kill the child and Red Hawk when I killed him." Gray Wolf said.

Gray Wolf fell silent and waited for Talking Bear's anger to sweep over him.

"You killed Snow Beaver to stop him from killing Red Hawk, is that what you are saying?" He asked.

"I was ordered to watch Red Hawk not kill him. To show Two Stars that you had not ordered it I killed Snow Beaver."

Gray Wolf expected a lot of yelling from Talking Bear but he never expected to hear laughter.

"You did well Gray Wolf not only will Two Stars trust me again so will Red Hawk." Talking Bear smiled then ordered him to leave.

"Master Adam, we won't be able to see them Indians much longer." George said pointing at the setting sun.

"He's right pa." John said as he reached for his gun and headed out the door. While Little Dove cared for Emma, Two Stars was holding a crying Rose in her arms. Red Hawk took one last look at Emma before he walked out behind them. Red Hawk stopped and watched as John and James headed to the back of the cabin while Adam and George headed to the front of it. All four men hadn't even noticed that Red Hawk wasn't behind them anymore. He chose to go to his place under the big tree and sat there instead.

"Do you think Red Hawk was right about Talking Bear is going to leave us alone now?" James asked.

John was quiet until the two of them had sat down before he gave James a reply to his question.

"Two Stars thinks that Talking Bear is more frightened of the baby than he is of Rose."

"At first I just thought she was just being a worried mother to be but now I think she is right to be frightened." John told him.

"Is she still alive?" Liz asked as her and Ruth joined Little Dove at Emma's bed.

"Is there anything we can do to help?" Ruth asked even before Little Dove could answer Liz's question.

Little Dove knew that the worried and crying women wasn't going to be much help. She understood the mothers need to help her child.

"You can get me some warm water in a bow and a soft cloth." Little Dove said pointing toward the other room.

She gave them the feeling of helping while she looked after Emma. After she had been brought the cloth and water Little Dove began to clean the wound on Emma's head. Little Dove had left a lot of the water in the cloth and when she placed it on the wound Emma opened her eyes.

"Two Stars go get Red Hawk." Little Dove said as she looked at Emma's opened eyes.

Emma could feel her eyes open but all she could see was darkness.

"Is it night?" She asked as she brought her hands to her eyes.

"She's awake." Little Dove said as Red Hawk dropped to his knees beside Emma's bed.

Emma could hear people around her but didn't know who was making the sounds. Her loud screams came more from not knowing who the people were than from the darkness. It wasn't until Emma heard Red Hawk say it's me that she stopped her screaming. Emma felt Red Hawk put his arms around her and pull her crying head to his chest.

"I can't see Red Hawk; I can't see." Emma kept saying over and over as she stared at him crying.

Emma couldn't see the tears that flowed from her eyes but she could feel them. Everyone in the room looked at each other in shock but didn't say a word. Liz dropped to her knees beside Emma's bed crying out to God to save her baby's eyes and to take hers instead.

You could see the fear on George's face when he and Master Adam saw Red Hawk running from the cabin. Both men thought that Emma had just died or he saw something they hadn't; either way it was bad news. Adam headed after Red Hawk while George went toward the cabin.

John and James had reached Red Hawk by the time Adam had caught up with him.

"What happened?" John was asking as Adam walked up.

"Emma has lost her sight." He told them as he got on his horse.

"What are we going to do?" James asked in a puzzling voice.

"You are not going to do anything!" Red Hawk yelled from the back of his horse.

"If one of you are seen at the village Talking Bear will have the excuse to kill you all."

"Do you understand what I'm saying?" Red Hawk asked while looking at John.

"Won't they kill you too if you go there?" James asked. "In the village he will have to take me before the village elders first." Red Hawk said as he rode off.

Talking Bear smiled at the thought of what Gray Wolf had said about Snow Beaver killing the slave girl before he killed him. That took care of one threat to the blood line now all he had to do was kill the whites and Two Starz's baby. Finding a reason to kill the whites wasn't going to be any trouble he was sure. His troubles would begin when someone found out that he was responsible for the death of a tribal Chief. As Chief Talking Bear was over everything outside the village but the elders was over the village. Even Talking Bear had to answer to the elders in the village. If the elders even had a suspicion he killed Two Starz's baby it would cost him his life. Talking Bear loved Two Stars but he wasn't going to let her taunt the tribal blood either.

If I can get rid of the baby without Two Stars knowing I did it, it could save her life.

Little Dove ran toward where the men stood watching Red Hawk ride away. "Where is he going?" She asked in a tone that showed her fear for her brother.

"He said he was going to talk to someone at the village." James told Little Dove.

"The village elder," John added as Little Dove looked at him.

"Red Hawk, come back!" Little Dove yelled as she chased him on foot. They all watched as Red Hawk reappeared and rode up to her.

"Getting yourself killed by Talking Bear isn't going to help that girl in there." Little Dove said pointing at the cabin.

"If you truly love her, stay with her now."

"No brother of mine would leave his women just when she needs him the most." Little Dove told him.

Two Stars got there just in time to see Red Hawk getting off the horse.

"I'm glad she talked him out of going to the village or he may have gotten us all killed." John said as he placed his hand on Two Starz's big belly.

"She hasn't talked Red Hawk out of going he has just put it off a while." Two Stars told John.

It had been a month and Talking Bear hadn't given them any more trouble. All the men were setting out in front of the cabin talking.

"Red Hawk, do you think that Talking Bear will leave us alone from now on?" James asked.

"I don't think we are being watched anymore." John added as his eyes scanned the tree line.

"If Gray Wolf is the one watching us you won't see him." Red Hawk said as he to scanned the trees.

"If this Gray Wolf is so good why was Snow Beaver the one to take your place instead of him?" John asked.

"I'm the reason that Gray Wolf was held down from that job." Red Hawk told the men around him.

He turned to face James before he went on.

"Gray Wolf wanted to marry Little Dove and he needed my permission."

"I would not give it and I had Talking Bear keep him where he was for a favor." Red Hawk said.

"Did Little Dove want to marry him?" James asked in a low voice. "No she liked him but she didn't want him for her mate." Red Hawk told James.

With each step Two Stars took toward John the weaker she became. She just had reached the group of men when her water broke covering her feet and the ground around them.

"John what's happening?" Two Stars was able to ask before she fell into his arms.

"Pa what's wrong with her?" John was asking as he picked Two Stars up and headed for the cabin.

"I'd say she is about to have your baby." Adam said laughingly as he watched John go.

"Hope it's a girl, I always wanted a girl." Adam said more to himself than to anyone else.

Red Hawk couldn't believe these men still didn't understand that if Two Stars had a girl the village couldn't save them anymore.

"The only thing that would keep Talking Bear from killing them was if Two Stars has a Chief."

"You had better hope that the baby is a boy seeing as to how that is the only thing that's keeping you alive now." Red Hawk said as he turned to go.

"I'm starting to wonder if these whites are worth the trouble of keeping alive." Red Hawk asked himself as he walked away from them.

"Master Adam if what Master Red Hawk say is true then we best be wishing for a boy." George told Adam as he watched Red Hawk go.

"What's going on?" Little Dove asked as she watched as John packed Two Stars through the door.

Little Dove was frightened for her friend because she knew that the baby wasn't due for another month. Little Dove had brought babies into this world before but the others were full term. If something went wrong Two Stars would never forgive her.

"Emma you are going to have to move off the bed." Liz was saying as she guided Emma to the bear skin rug in the corner.

"What's going on maw?" Emma asked as she took her seat on the bear skin.

"It's miss Two Stars she's having her baby." Liz said as she took a seat beside Emma.

"I want all you men to get out of here." Ruth said as she pushed John toward the cabin door.

John took one last look at Two Stars as he went out the door and headed for the men. The whole time he walked he kept looking over his shoulder at the cabin.

Gray Wolf had just arrived to watch the whites for the night when he noticed how the men were acting strange. He got as close as he dared to get so he could hear what they were saying. Gray Wolf had been watching the cabin when he heard all the men yelling so loud he knew that something was going on. Once he was close enough he heard them talking about Two Stars having her baby.

"They are killing her." Rose said as she locked her arms around Emma and hid her face in Emma's chest.

"No they're not Rose she is just having a baby is all." Emma said to Rose as she cradled her in her arms.

"Just think Rose in just a few hours we will have our own baby to play with." Emma said with a laugh.

Rose's eyes became as big as they could get when she decided to look once more at Two Stars.

She watched in horror as Two Stars let out a cry as Little Dove held the baby upside down and slapped it on its butt. The baby's cries filled the room and brought a smile to Emma's face.

Emma's ears weren't the only ears that heard the baby's cries. Gray Wolf also heard them and decided that he must get closer to hear the sex of the child.

Gray Wolf had to know if it was a girl or was it a new born tribal Chief.

When John heard the cries he started to head for the cabin until Adam got him by the arm.

"You had better wait until they call you son." Adam said still holding onto John's arm.

"Master John I watched my Liz birth a lot of babies and it's not a pretty sight." George said and smiled.

Gray Wolf had to leave not knowing the sex of the child when he saw Red Hawk headed toward him. Red Hawk watched in amazement as the white men looked toward the cabin and told John of the good job he had done. Gray Wolf used this time to make his way to his horse and to get away. If it hadn't been for the horse making a loud sound they would never had known that Gray Wolf had ever been there.

"Talking Bear knows about the baby now." Red Hawk said as he watched Gray Wolf ride away toward the village.

"What will he do?" Adam asked as he to watched Gray Wolf ride off.

"He doesn't know the child's sex yet." Red Hawk said as he looked once more at the cabin.

Talking Bear stood at the entrance to his teepee and looked once more in the direction of Two Starz's cabin. He thought that he should have heard something from Gray Wolf by now. Talking Bear had been keeping a close watch on Two Stars here lately. If he had counted it right she should be getting very close to the time the baby was due. Talking Bear had no more than stepped through the opening of the teepee when Gray Wolf rode into the village. He didn't stop the horse until he was at the Chief's teepee.

Talking Bear had just taken a toke of his pipe when Gray Wolf came in.

"Two Stars is having her baby." Were his first words to Talking Bear.

Talking Bear started choking as he blew out the smoke from the pipe. Talking Bear dropped the pipe on the ground as he jumped to his feet.

"Dose it live?" Talking Bear asked once he had made it to his feet.

"Yes." Gray Wolf said with a smile I heard it crying as I rode away.

"Is it a boy?" Was Talking Bears next question.

The smile left Gray Wolf's face as he had to tell Talking Bear that he didn't know what the sex of the child was.

"Tell no one about this." Talking Bear ordered just as Gold Eagle entered the teepee.

Gold Eagle was the head of the five elders that run the village. "The old spirit reader said he saw the birth of a Chief; is this true?" Gold Eagle asked Talking Bear.

Just as the smile returned to Gray Wolf's face when he started to tell Gold Eagle the truth, Talking Bear stopped him.

"Two Starz's baby isn't due for another moon but I'll send Gray Wolf to see." Talking Bear said as he walked Gold Eagle to the door of the teepee.

"You will tell me when the Chief is born?" Gold Eagle asked as he walked out.

"Gold Eagle you will be the first to know." Talking Bear was saying as he left.

Gray Wolf couldn't believe what he had just heard Talking Bear do; lie to the village elder. Not just any village elder either Gold Eagle, head of the elders. In the village Gold Eagle holds more power than Talking Bear and for him to lie to him could mean his death as well as

Talking Bear's.

"I guess you are asking yourself why I just lied to Gold Eagle." Talking Bear stated as he walked back to where Gray Wolf stood.

"Gold Eagle is head of the village he could have us both killed, if not cast us out of the village." Gray Wolf said with fear in his voice.

"I didn't say that Two Stars didn't have her baby I just said that she wasn't due yet." Talking Bear said as if it made the lie any better.

"Look Gray Wolf if you want to be my number one you will never tell anyone about this." Talking Bear said.

"Now I want you to go back to the cabin and find out what the child is, a boy or a girl."

Talking Bear said as he walked Gray Wolf to the door.

Gray Wolf gave one last look at Talking Bear who was standing at the teepee door as he got on his horse. Gray Wolf hadn't liked the way Talking Bear had put his life in danger just now but he was the Chief.

The sound of the baby crying made John forget all about Adam's and George's worrying and he ran toward the cabin. By the time John reached the door the babies cries suddenly stopped all at once making fear shoot through John. Little Dove handed the baby to Two Stars and she was trying to get the baby to feed. Two Stars took her breast and placed the nipple to the baby's mouth but he didn't suck it.

"Squeeze your nipple and place the milk to his mouth." Ruth told her with a smile.

As soon as the baby got the first drop of milk in his mouth he started sucking the breast for all it had. A tear made its way down Two Starz's cheek as she watched the new tribal Chief take his first meal.

"I wish I could see him." Emma said as she and Rose sat and could hear the others talking.

"I'll go see." Rose said as she got to her feet and walked over to where she could see better.

The baby was so small that it didn't look real to Rose. She remembered having a doll that was bigger than that baby.

Gray Wolf had managed to get close enough to the cabin to hear that the baby was a boy.

As he slowly made his way back to his horse Gray Wolf's thoughts were on the new tribal Chief. He also thought of what Talking Bear was going to do once he told him of the boy. Gray Wolf rode into the village and the first person he met was Gold Eagle.

"Is it born yet?" He asked as Gray Wolf rode by him. Gray Wolf didn't answer him instead rode on passed him and straight to Talking Bear's teepee.

Talking Bear smiled when he saw Gray Wolf back so soon.

"Is it a boy?" Talking Bear asked as Gray Wolf entered the teepee.

"It's a boy Talking Bear the village has a new tribal Chief." Gray Wolf said proudly with a smile.

"He is not a Chief until I'm dead and don't you forget that." Talking Bear said angrily.

"I meant no disrespect Talking Bear." Gray Wolf said quickly.

"I know you didn't." Talking Bear said in a more calm voice.

"I must now ask you not to tell anyone else about this?" Talking Bear asked Gray Wolf.

Gray Wolf said, "No." With such conviction that Talking Bear new he was telling him the truth.

"You can't tell anyone about this Gray Wolf." Talking Bear said then stood and studied his reaction before going on.

"What I'm going to tell you to do is for the good of the village."

"If it's for the village shouldn't we tell Gold Eagle about it?"

Gray wolf asked. Gray Wolf felt a cold chill go up his back when Talking Bear said, "No I'll tell him when the time comes."

Talking Bear walked back and stood right in front of Gray Wolf before he said anything else.

"You will take three young braves from the shamed village and attack the cabin and the baby." Gray Wolf couldn't believe what he was hearing.

Talking Bear's words would mean not only the death of the new born Chief but his and Talking Bear's as well. Gray Wolf tried his best to tell Talking Bear that it would be foolish to attack the white guns with just three young braves.

"As soon as you have them capture the white's attention, you can get to the boy and kill him. I'll be waiting with a hundred braves then we can kill them all." Talking Bear said as he stared blankly at the door.

The next morning John noticed Red Hawk staring at the sun as it made its way up higher and higher into the sky. Once Red Hawk saw John he called him over then turned back toward the village.

"I'm sure Talking Bear knows by now that the baby is a new Chief and he will try to kill him." Red Hawk said without looking at him.

"You said the village would protect him." John said loudly as Adam reached them.

"If Gold Eagle knows about the baby he will be safe but if Talking Bear didn't tell him the Chief is still in danger."

By this time both James and George had joined the three men.

"No matter where they come from it will be the baby that he is after." Red Hawk said as he walked away toward the woods.

"Where are you going?" John asked.

"To protect my Chief." Red Hawk said as he vanished into the woods.

"What did he mean by that John?" James asked with a trace of fear in his voice.

"I hope he meant that he was still on our side." John said as he stared where Red Hawk had disappeared into the trees.

As Gray Wolf and the three braves left the village they were surprised to see Gold Eagle sitting on his horse with ten braves there in front of them. The three young braves couldn't understand the smile that appeared on Gray Wolf's face.

"Was the baby a boy?" Gold Eagle asked as Gray Wolf reached him.

This time Gray Wolf knew he couldn't just shake his head and go on.

"Yes Gold Eagle it's a new Chief." Gray Wolf said as he stopped in front of him.

"Red Hawk came to me and said that Talking Bear is trying to have the baby killed, is this true?" Gold Eagle asked.

Gray Wolf knew that Gold Eagle already knew the answer even before he had asked him. Even before Gray Wolf had time to say a word Gold Eagle pointed at the three young braves behind Gray Wolf.

"This is what Talking Bear has sent to kill, a Chief?" Gold Eagle asked.

"Talking Bear thinks by killing the boy he will keep the blood of the people pure." Gray Wolf said louder than he wanted.

Gray Wolf saw the anger cover Gold Eagle's face.

"The day that Iron Bear gave Two Stars to Gain the blood of the tribe became his blood." Gold Eagle said angrily.

"Every brave in the village will die for him if that is what it takes."

Talking Bear saw Gray Wolf talking too Gold Eagle as he came out of his teepee to get his war party. Talking Bear knew that Gray Wolf had told Gold Eagle everything by now so he made his way out of the village alone. Talking Bear knew that as soon as the village learned what he tried to do he was as good as dead. He decided if he was going to be killed by Gold Eagle he would die trying to kill the boy. With the boy dead his girls stood a chance of being the mother of the next tribal Chief.

Talking Bear made his way slowly toward the cabin to where he could see everyone. He could see all the men except Red Hawk and that worried him. As Talking Bear reached the back of the cabin he could hear the baby cries from inside. Talking Bear waited until the men had their backs to him then made his way to the cabin door. He pulled his knife then threw all his weight on the door as he went through it. The first thing he saw was Two Stars as she held the baby to her breast. It wasn't until he heard the sound of the hammer being pulled back on a gun that he saw Red Hawk. The look on Talking Bear's face told Red Hawk that he had come too far to stop now. As Talking Bear raised the knife and stepped toward the bed Red Hawk pulled the trigger. The gun let out a loud noise as Talking Bear saw the cloud of smoke chase the ball from the gun. As if the bullet was going so slow he could stop it Talking Bear put out his hand to catch it before it hit his chest. He knew he had failed when he felt it tearing its way to his heart. Red Hawk dropped the gun and it hit the floor the same time Talking Bear did. They all watched as Red Hawk dropped to his knees beside him.

At least fifty braves had joined Gold Eagle and Gray Wolf at the cabin by now. Gray Wolf showed that his hands carried no threat as he reached Adam and John. They all heard the sound that the gun made at the same time. The sound had told Gray Wolf that Talking Bear had made it into the cabin. The sound also told him that Talking Bear was dead. When John and Adam heard the sound they both ran for the cabin leaving George and James there with the Indians. The first thing John saw as he burst through was Talking Bear's dead body lying on the floor. His eyes next moved to Two Stars lying frozen in the bed with the baby in one hand and a knife in the other. Two Stars dropped the knife so she could wipe away the tears that blocked the sight of her brother's body on the floor. Two Stars handed the crying baby to Little Dove who was just as stunned as Two Stars. They all watched in silence as Two Stars made her way through the smoke from the shot to drop down beside Red Hawk. She saw that Red Hawk couldn't hide the tears that he spilled for his friend as well. Red Hawk rose to his feet as John came toward them and stopped John before he reached Two Stars.

"Leave her too say goodbye to her brother." Red Hawk said as he led the men outside.

The young braves didn't know what the sound from inside the cabin meant. They became very frightened and started preparing for battle. No matter where George looked he saw Indians and they were getting closer.

"Master James we had better put these on the ground." He said as he put his gun down.

James placed his gun down as the one called Gray Wolf got off his horse. The one called Gold Eagle turned to the young braves and stopped their fears. Gold Eagle could understand English very well but he couldn't speak it. When he started speaking in his native tongue neither James nor George could understand what he was saying. Gray Wolf saw that the two men didn't understand what Gold Eagle was saying so he began translating for them.

"This is the village Chief, Gold Eagle; he has come to protect the new born Chief." Gray Wolf said as he pointed toward Gold Eagle.

"He has come to name the new Chief and to take him to the village." Gray Wolf went on to say.

When James could understand what was being said his eyes went to where he had laid his gun.

Both James and George sighed a breath of relief when they saw Red Hawk and the others come out of the cabin.

"Master Red Hawk you had better talk to theses Indians before they start killing us all." George said in a panic.

"You don't need to worry about that Indian." Red Hawk said as he reached him.

Gray Wolf saw a smile come to Gold Eagle's face as Red Hawk reached him.

"Talking Bear is dead for trying to kill the new Chief." Red Hawk said as he reached where Gold Eagle and Gray Wolf stood.

"I have come to name the new Chief." Gold Eagle said as Red Hawk stopped in front of him.

"The new Chief is safe Gold Eagle; with the help of the whites Talking Bear was not able to kill him."

Gold Eagle turned his eyes toward the cabin before he spoke. Gold Eagle turned his eyes back to Red Hawk as he spoke in a loud enough voice for all the braves to hear.

"I was unaware of Talking Bear's feelings toward the new Chief. Let it be known that Talking Bear has set the cost for attempting to harm the new Chief. I have come to take the new Chief and Two Stars back to the village." Gold Eagle said in a voice that told Red Hawk that he wouldn't take no for a reply.

"What of the others?" Red Hawk asked as he looked at Gray Wolf and fifty braves behind him.

"That will all be up to Two Stars." Red Hawk told Gold Eagle as he kept his eyes on Gray Wolf's eyes for the slightest change in them.

Red Hawk watched as he saw Gray Wolf's eyes grow wide. As Red

Hawk turned to see what he was looking at the sight of four guns sticking out came into view.

"They are only protecting their own just as you are; they will not kill you unless I tell them to." Red Hawk told Gray wolf.

Gray Wolf had no doubt that every word that Red Hawk said was true. "Put the guns down before coming over here." Red Hawk told John as he kept his eyes on the young braves behind Gray Wolf and Gold Eagle.

Both Adam and John slowly placed their guns on the ground before walking to where Red Hawk stood.

"This is Gold Eagle; he is the village elder he has brought these braves to protect the new Chief." Red Hawk paused before he went on.

"Gold Eagle came to take Two Stars and the new Chief Back to the village to protect them."

"While they are Gold Eagle will name the new Chief."

Red Hawk saw John start shaking his head no.

"Neither Two Stars nor the baby are going anywhere." John said as he turned to Gold Eagle.

"You don't understand." Red Hawk said as he pointed a finger at the braves behind Gold Eagle.

"He will protect the new Chief from anyone even you. It will be up to Two Stars if she wants to go but the baby must be named by the village elder at the village."

John's eyes turned toward the cabin.

"Did Two Stars know about this?" John asked as he stared at the cabin. Red Hawk looked at John in a puzzled look for asking such a question.

"Everyone in the village knows that law." Red Hawk said still looking confused.

That explains why Two Stars would change the subject when he asked her what they were going to name the baby.

John didn't realize he was talking out loud as he stared at the cabin until Red Hawk asked him, "what?"

John wanted to tell Gold Eagle that he was going to give the baby his name but to do so he could get them all killed so he kept quiet. No matter what name the village gave him his name to John would always be David.

"There she is." Gray Wolf said pointing toward the cabin.

All eyes turned to see Two Stars being helped out onto the porch by Little Dove. John started to go to her but as he started Red Hawk reached out his hand and stopped him.

"You cannot interfere." Red Hawk said as he stopped John.

John stood and watched in silence as Two Starz's legs grew weaker the closer to Gold Eagle she got. She dropped to her knees in front of him then raised the baby up to him.

"I give my people a new Chief." She said without looking up.

Gold Eagle reached down and took the baby from Two Starz's hands. There was no sound from anyone as he raised the boy above his head.

"Oh great Spirit I give to you a new Chief." Gold Eagle said then paused and looked at John.

"His name will be Spotted Bear from now on."

Two Stars raised her head and looked at her new Chief for the first time. John couldn't explain the feeling of pride for his son even though he was now known as Spotted Bear. With Little Doves help Two Stars rose to her feet and stood in front of Gold Eagle.

"I will bring Spotted Bear and show him his people in a few days." She said.

"I will be staying here until then with my other family."

"Then I will leave these braves here to protect Spotted Bear." Gold Eagle said pointing at the braves behind him.

Two Stars knew that Gold Eagle wasn't going to leave and not have braves watching over Spotted Bear.

"Then I'll take that one." She said pointing at Gray Wolf.

Red Hawk was just as surprised as Gray Wolf when Two Stars pointed at Gray Wolf.

"Then you will stay here Gray Wolf." Gold Eagle said as he got back on his horse.

"Master Adam does this mean them Indians will leave us alone now?" George asked not taking his eyes off Gray Wolf.

"Yes George I think your right." Adam said as they all watched the last brave leave their sight.

As soon as the last brave was gone Two Stars handed Little Dove Spotted Bear and fell into John's arms.

"Does you need help Master John?" George asked as he watched John swoop Two Stars up into his arms and head for the cabin.

Without a word John just shook his head no then hurried away.

"George you go ahead of them and get that dead Indian out of there." Adam ordered pointing toward the cabin.

"Wait up Master John and let me get that out of there." George said as he stopped at the door.

"Oh my." Rose said as she saw John packing Two Stars through the door.

"What's going on?" Emma asked when she heard the noise.

"They done killed the Indian lady." She said with fear in her voice.

Unsure as to what was going on Emma suddenly grew as frightened as Rose. Rose lost her fear when she saw John let go of Two Starz's feet and they dropped to the floor. When Rose became very quiet it only made Emma's fear grow even stronger.

"Is Red Hawk here?" Emma asked now worried that he may have been killed too.

Little Dove heard Emma's question and sat down beside her and took her by the hand.

"Both Red Hawk and Two Stars are alive and well. My brother is outside with the men and Master John has put Two Stars back to bed."

Emma smiled as Little Dove gave her hand a gentle squeeze before letting go of it.

After putting Two Stars on the bed John kissed her on the forehead then walked outside and rejoined the rest of the men. John could hear George's question as he walked up to them.

He heard him say, "Master Adam does you think we'll be alright now?" George asked.

"I think so George but you should ask this man here." Adam said as he saw Red Hawk coming.

"How about it Red Hawk are we going to be safe now?" John asked once Red Hawk reached them.

"You will be safe as long as Spotted Bear lives." He told them.

"At sunrise I will go to the village and talk to Gold Eagle. He will decide who is to be Chief until Spotted Bear grows up to be a man." Red Hawk said then left.

"Tomorrow we will go back and rebuild Fort Huff and our homes." Adam told them as he stared back toward the old camp.

Gold Eagle sat with the other two elders trying to decide who was going to be the next Chief. One of the elders wanted Gray Wolf as the next Chief and the other wanted Red Hawk.

Gold Eagle knew that Gray Wolf could be trusted but Red Hawk had a lot more years going for him. Iron Bird sat in Gray Wolf's teepee staring out the door at the teepee where the village elders were meeting.

"Who do you think they will pick?" Iron Bird asked without taking his eyes from the door.

Gray Wolf also looked at the teepee before he spoke.

"In the elders' eyes I have always came in behind Red Hawk there is no reason for that to change." Gray Wolf said as he took his eyes off the door.

"If Red Hawk becomes Chief I will not serve him." Iron Bird said more to himself than to Gray Wolf.

Gray Wolf jumped to his feet and Iron Bird could see how angry his words had made Gray Wolf.

"If Red Hawk is chosen you will serve him." He yelled.

Spotted Bear started crying loudly as he laid beside his mother. What worried Little Dove was the sound didn't wake Two Stars at all.

Little Dove hoped her friend was just tired and not from the loss of blood. She picked up Spotted Bear and tried to get him to stop crying by walking him around but it didn't work.

"The child is hungry." Ruth said as she pointed toward Two Stars.

Little Dove handed the baby to Ruth while she took off Two Starz's dress so the boy could suck.

As soon as Spotted Bear chased down the nipple with his mouth he never made another sound.

Little Dove waited until the boy had gotten his fill and he fell asleep before she laid him down beside Two Stars. She then walked over and sat down beside Emma and Rose on the bear skin.

"Emma I'm going to take a look at your eyes now so don't be frightened ok." Little Dove told her.

"I'm not afraid of you Little Dove, you are Red Hawk's sister and now you are my sister." Emma told her.

If Emma could have seen Little Dove's face like Rose did, she would have seen the smile on it.

"My brother has chosen well in a mate." Little Dove said as she placed a hand on Emma's head.

"What about me?" Rose asked as she tugged at Little Dove's dress.

"It's a fact that you have stolen Red Hawk's heart little one." Little Dove said as she took Rose by the hand and squeezed it.

"You want to hear something funny?" Emma asked.

Even before anyone could say a word she went on.

"The first time that I felt free was the day Red Hawk saw me naked at the creek."

The words naked at the creek sent a cold chill up Rose's back as she remembered the sight she saw the day she was brought here. The thought of James and John standing in that creek without clothing still frightened her. The sound of Spotted Bear's crying jerked Little Dove's attention back to Two Stars and the baby. As Little Dove reached the side of the bed she was glad to find that it was no more than a baby who had lost his nipple.

Just as the morning sun made its way up to erase the darkness. John stood staring at the path leading to the place that would become Ft. Huff. John had so many thoughts going through his head at one time he didn't know where to start. He had been so caught up in his thoughts that he didn't notice Adam walking up behind him.

"What you studying on so hard?" Adam asked once he reached him.

"I was just wondering if we will need to build a fort now pa seeing that Talking Bear is dead." John said.

"Talking Bear or not we need the fort more now than before." Adam said loudly.

"Red Hawk seems to think that if Gray Wolf becomes the new Chief we will still be safe."

Red Hawk seemed to just appear out of nowhere.

"Do we still need to build the fort?" John asked even before Red Hawk reached him.

"You build what you want, just because Talking Bear is dead doesn't mean your life or Spotted Bear are out of danger." Red Hawk said angrily.

Just as Red Hawk mounted his horse to leave he paused and looked at John.

"Do not under estimate Gray Wolf." He said then left.

"What did he mean by that?" James asked as he to stood by John watching Red Hawk ride away.

"He means dear brother we have got a fort to build." John said as he turned and walked away.

Adam placed a hand on James's shoulder before he spoke.

"As soon as you and George get done with your eating start gathering up what tools we have left and put them in the wagon." Adam told him.

"Sure pa as soon as we finish eating we'll do that." James said as Adam took away his hand and walked away.

"I don't see why we still need a fort now that John is the Chief's pa." James said as he sat down beside George to eat.

"Now Master James you knows that your pa and Master John has done figured them Indians out."

"They knows that we will be needing that fort someday." George said loudly.

"I suppose your right George." James was saying as he took his seat.

George liked the idea of a fort that is why he was glad Adam was going ahead and building it. If they had built one the first time maybe Emma would still have her eyes he thought.

As Red Hawk rode into the village that morning he noticed how everyone seemed to be staring at him. Red Hawk had to admit he didn't like the feeling it gave him. He had been sent word by Gold Eagle to be there but he had not been told why. Red Hawk had a feeling it had something to do with Gray Wolf. If it was Gold Eagle's way of telling him that Gray Wolf was now chief it was ok with him. Red Hawk stopped his horse outside the council teepee and went in. As soon as Red Hawk entered the teepee a young warrior was sent to get Gray Wolf.

"Sit there Red Hawk." Gold Eagle said pointing to a spot in front of the other village elders.

"When Gray Wolf gets here I will tell you who we have decided will become our new Chief."

Red Hawk didn't have long to wait before Gray Wolf appeared.

"The council had a hard time in making its decision between you." Gold Eagle said as Gray Wolf took his seat beside Red Hawk.

"Red Hawk you will be Chief." Gold Eagle said.

As Liz held Spotted Bear for the first time she noticed how he smiled even though he was asleep. He must be knowing that he is free Liz thought to herself as she stared at Spotted Bear.

When Liz took her eyes off of the baby she turned them toward Emma. Her sight had been lost but had gained her freedom. The sound of Master John as he came through the door drew Liz's thoughts away from Emma. She watched as he walked over to where Little Dove sat on Two Starz's bed.

"Is she going to be alright?" he was asking even before he stopped.

"I wished I could tell you that she was but tribal law says I must tell you the truth."

"No she isn't getting better but she isn't getting worse." Little Dove said as they looked at Two Stars lying there.

"There is got to be something we can do for her." John said a little louder than he wanted too.

It surprised John when Little Dove shot up off the bed right in his face.

"Go and let her rest is the best thing!" She yelled.

Without a word John took a look at Two Stars then turned and walked out. As he took a step off the porch he saw Red Hawk returning from the village. He changed his direction and walked toward him. The early morning air had a chill to it here lately and John could see his own breath as he spoke.

"Did Gold Eagle tell you anything?" John asked as Red Hawk got off the horse.

"I come to take Emma to the village with me." Red Hawk told John. "You can't do that Red Hawk, she would be in danger, you told me yourself!" John yelled.

Red Hawk could hear the real fear in John's voice so he placed his hand on John's shoulder before he spoke.

"You will not have to worry about the tribal Chief anymore." Red Hawk said then pointed at himself.

"They made you the Chief?" John asked just out of reflex.

"Yes and I have the full help of the village elders." Red Hawk said as he took his hand off John's shoulder.

"No one will hurt Emma again." Red Hawk said.

Emma couldn't see the people looking at her but she could feel them as she and Red Hawk rode into the village. Red Hawk could feel their eyes on them as well as he stopped the horse and got off first so that he could help Emma down. The young women of the village began to reach out to touch Emma just to make sure she was real. Red

Hawk knew that they meant Emma no harm but he ran them away anyway. He could also tell by the expressions on the brave's faces who was glad to see him and who wasn't. Seeing that Red Hawk was paying more attention to the braves than the girls Two Feathers made her way back to where Emma stood. Slowly she reached out a hand and placed it on Emma's face feeling the texture of Emma's skin.

"Two Feathers get away from her!" Red Hawk yelled.

"No Red Hawk let her." Emma told him."

I'm just as curious as she is." Emma said reaching out her hand.

It wasn't until Two Feathers looked at Emma's eyes that she realized Emma couldn't see. Red Hawk watched as Two Feathers took Emma's hand and placed it on her face as well.

"You're very pretty." Emma said as she dragged her finger tips down Two feathers' face.

Emma was surprised when Two Feathers said, "So are you." In plain English. "I must be going." Two Feathers said in a different tone as she pushed Emma's hand away.

"No wait." Emma said as she waved her hand through the air for the slightest touch of the girl.

The sight of Flying Doe, Gold Eagle's wife, coming toward them sent Two Feathers off in a run.

The next sound Emma could hear was the voice of a woman who spoke only Shawnee.

"Is this your new woman?" Flying Doe asked as she reached Emma and Red Hawk.

Emma couldn't understand a word the woman was saying but she knew by the way Red Hawk answered her she was a woman of power.

"What does she want?" Emma was asking while Red Hawk was trying to answer Flying Doe.

"She only wants to know if you come to the village of your own free will." Red Hawk said.

My own free will Emma thought and said, "Yes."

"Then the people accept you as our people." Flying Doe told Emma then left.

"What did she mean?" Emma asked Red Hawk.

"She is saying that you are now accepted as one of the tribe." He said then smiled.

Emma didn't know why but being told she now belonged to the tribe made her feel good. It was at that moment that Emma felt like the chains of slavery was broken. For the first time in her life Emma felt free. Red Hawk called for Two Feathers to come and take Emma to his teepee and stay with her.

"I must go and talk to Gold Eagle." Red Hawk said as Two Feathers led her away.

Gray Wolf was already sitting with the elders when Red Hawk entered the teepee.

Red Hawk stood in front of the three elders and turned toward Gray Wolf before he said anything.

"I will do my best as the Chief to protect Spotted Bear and the tribe." Red Hawk said as he turned his eyes back to the elders.

Gray Wolf rose to his feet and stood beside Red Hawk.

"I will follow and serve Red Hawk as I did Talking Bear." Gray Wolf said as he looked at Red Hawk.

"Then you will serve as my number one Gray Wolf." Red Hawk said as he turned to leave.

Gray Wolf never took his eyes off Red Hawk as he walked out.

"Must be going to see the slave girl." Gold Eagle said as he too was watching Red Hawk leave.

Gray Wolf thought for the first time now what Talking Bear was so frightened of.

When Red Hawk saw Two Feathers and Emma talking a cold chill went down his back like he had been cut with ice. Two Feathers was one of Talking Bear's two daughters. He wondered if Emma had already told her that he was the one who killed Talking Bear.

"Red Hawk I think Two Feathers can talk to me as good as you." Emma said as Red Hawk reached them.

"You have done well but I will get Fire Fly to see after her now." Red Hawk said in a low voice after walking Two Feathers to the door.

"See you later." Emma said then laughed as she looked in Two Feathers direction.

Without a word Two Feathers turned her eyes toward Emma then back to Red Hawk then left.

Red Hawk walked back and sat down beside Emma before he spoke. "What did you and Two Feathers talk about?" He asked once he took his seat.

"Just girl things Red Hawk." Emma said in a playful tone.

"Just as you came in she was telling me about her father being killed in battle." Emma told him.

Red Hawk could tell by the way Emma talked that she didn't know that Two Feathers was talking about Talking Bear.

"Emma from now on I'm going to leave you with someone who is much older." Red Hawk said as he took Emma by the hand.

"But why Red Hawk?" Emma asked as she jerked her hand away from his.

"Two Feathers is just too young to care for you." Red Hawk told Emma as he took her hand back.

Emma remembered when they were at the creek and Red Hawk had asked her to trust him. Without her eyes Red Hawk was the only one she could trust she told herself.

"You know best but I sure liked Two Feathers." She said. "There are lots of girls for you to talk to." Red Hawk told Emma as he pulled her to her feet.

"I don't want a lot of girls to talk to, I want Two Feathers." Emma said as Red Hawk led her toward the door.

When Red Hawk saw tears roll down Emma's cheek he gave in to her. "I will send for her so you stay here until she gets here." Red Hawk said as he sat Emma back down.

Once Emma had gotten seated Red Hawk saw a smile come to her face as she wiped away her tears.

Red Hawk hadn't been gone long before Two Feathers came into the teepee. She had been so quiet that Emma didn't know she was there. Emma jumped as Two Feathers spoke.

"Red Hawk said you choose me." Two Feathers said as she stood before Emma.

"Yes I did." Emma said as she patted the ground beside her. "Now that Red Hawk is Chief you will find that most of the people will treat you with respect." Two Feathers was saying as she sat down.

"Of course I wouldn't be counting on much respect from my sister Blue Bird." Two Feathers said once she took her seat.

Two Feathers watched as the smile left Emma's face. "Why would your sister not like me?" Emma asked as she forced the smile back to her face.

"Well she doesn't have anything against you exactly it's that Red Hawk chose you over her."

"My sister Blue Bird has been in love with Red Hawk ever since we were little. She has tried to tell him but he just doesn't seem to catch on." Two Feathers said.

"You have nothing to worry about though as long as Red Hawk is Chief she will leave you alone."

Emma kept saying Blue Bird over and over in her head as she stared at the darkness.

What's it like to be a slave?" Two Feathers asked to break the silence. Emma had never thought of it like that before.

Her whole life had been spent in slavery and now that she was free she felt no different.

"Before I met Red Hawk I was a slave to life now I'm a slave to darkness." Emma told her.

Two Feathers closed her eyes and tried to feel with Emma the weight of her burden. Until now Two Feathers had taken her eyes for granted, until now that is.

Blue Bird sat and stared closely at Talking Bear's things that were scattered around the teepee. She reached over and picked up his pipe that he had left lying on the ground by his blanket. Red Hawk had stolen her life a long time before he killed her father she told herself as she laid the pipe back down. She remembered seeing him sitting at Talking Bear's side from the time she could walk. Even though she had saved herself for the day she became his mate he hadn't given her a second thought. Now she was told that he had killed her father and taken the slave girl for his mate. Blue Bird quickly jerked her hands to her face and tried to stop the tears from racing down her cheeks.

"What could she do to hurt Red Hawk as much as he had her?" She asked herself.

If she killed him then he would only hurt for a short time before he died. Only by letting him live could she make him suffer like her for the rest of his life.

"I will think of something." She told herself as she got to her feet and brushed the dirt from her dress.

Now that Emma was gone Rose seemed to follow Little Dove around like she had Emma.

At first Little Dove thought that it was like having a little girl of her own. After a few days it started to get to her. What time she spent taking care of Two Stars was one thing but when Rose followed her to meet James she had to draw the line. Any time the two of them managed to get any time to themselves, Rose seemed to be between them. The idea of taking Rose to the village to stay with Emma and Red Hawk had crossed her mind. Little Dove soon put that idea out of her head knowing the whites would never go for it. James wouldn't touch her as long as Rose was around and it seemed to Little Dove that she was always there. All it took was a sad look and a smile from Rose for Little Dove to realize she could never say anything to Rose.

"Where are you going?" Rose asked as Little Dove headed for the door.

Little Dove made sure that James was watching her before she answered her.

"For a walk so you stay here and watch over Two Stars for me." She told Rose.

The nights had become much cooler this time of year so Little Dove could see James breathing as he stood in the shadow of the outhouse. The full moon lite up the area so bright it looked more like day.

"If you were an Indian you would know not to breathe into the light." Little Dove said laughingly before she reached where James was hiding himself.

"Little Dove I need to see you." James was saying as he to stepped out into the light.

James's words seemed to frighten Little Dove; had he lost his sight she was asking herself.

"Have you lost your eyes? Do you not see me?" She asked once she had reached him.

"It has nothing to do with my eyes." James said as he reached out and took Little Dove by the arms.

"I can't get you out of my dreams." James said as he let go of her arms.

"I have missed you as well." She told him as she put her arms around him and hugged him.

"The little time I get away from Two Stars and your mother I have Rose with me." She told him.

"Yah, I've noticed how she has stayed with you since Emma has gone." James said as he put his arms around Little Dove as well then kissed her.

Blue Bird would walk back and forth from the door to her bed watching for Two Feathers to come home from Red Hawk's teepee. She was in a hurry to find out as much about the slave girl as she could. At first Blue Bird was mad at Two Feathers for staying with the slave girl then she thought of all the help Two Feathers could be to her. Blue Bird had been the one that had told Two Feathers that their father had been killed in battle so she had no hate in her heart for Red Hawk. Blue Bird's hate for him was enough for them both.

It was getting dark outside by the time Two Feathers came home. "Where have you been?" She asked loudly as Two Feathers came through the door.

"I have been talking to Red Hawk's woman like I was told to do."

She said in a tone that matched Blue Birds.

Blue Bird knew that if she got Two Feathers mad at her she wouldn't get what she wanted from her.

"Don't get mad I was just worried about you out there in the dark." Blue Bird told her.

"I think that I was safe enough with a blind girl." Two Feathers said in a tone that told Blue Bird that she didn't believe her.

Two Feathers watched a look of anger cross Blue Bird's face.

"What do you mean a blind girl?" Blue Bird asked.

"I mean that Red Hawk's woman is blind as a bat." Two Feathers said as she closed her eyes to show Blue Bird what she meant.

Blue Bird could hide her anger no longer. Red Hawk had chosen a blind slave girl over her was more than she could stand.

"Emma is part of the people now and she is my good friend." Two Feathers told her sister.

"Well she is no friend of mine." Blue Bird shot back loudly.

"What is the matter with you?" Two Feathers asked being confused by her sister's anger toward Emma.

"You're mad at her because she got Red Hawk instead of you; aren't you?" Two Feathers asked.

Blue Bird turned her back to her so she couldn't see the tears falling from her eyes.

"You don't have to like her but you had better remember that she is Red Hawk's woman." Two Feathers told Blue Bird and then walked away.

It was about daybreak when Spotted Bear started crying for his breakfast very loudly. Little Dove woke to find that Rose was lying behind her with her arm thrown over her. She gently lifted the little arm and placed it off of her as to not wake her. Little Dove was surprised to see Two Stars sitting up and putting her nipple into the baby's mouth.

"Our big Chief is hungry this morning." Two Stars said as Little Dove reached the bed.

"How do you feel?" Little Dove asked.

"I think that I'm just as hungry as he is." Two Stars said nodding her head toward Spotted Bear who was sucking her breast for all it had.

Little Dove reached out and placed her hand on Two Starz's head to check her fever and found none.

"I'll fix you something to eat." Little Dove said as she smiled and headed for the fireplace.

The darkness that filled the cabin was broken by Liz as she put a match to the lamp. Rose awoke to the sound of the women talking so loudly that it frightened her. Seeing that it was nothing she rolled over and went back to sleep.

Emma's heart pounded hard in her breast when Red Hawk returned and sent Two Feathers away leaving her alone with him for the first time. Not knowing the feelings of a woman before Emma had depended on the safety of Master John and Master James until now. She could feel Red Hawk's presents but without her eyes she couldn't tell what he was thinking. When Red Hawk looked at Emma he could see her fear show on her face.

"Have no fear Emma, I will not hurt you." Red Hawk said as he took her in both arms and pulled her into his chest.

"I will wait for you to come to me." He said once her head laid there.

Emma eased her head off of Red Hawk's chest and turned to face him.

"Red Hawk I have given myself to you freely I have been drawn to you since you caught me taking a bath at the creek." Emma said and kissed him.

Emma's hand shook slightly as she rose to her feet and began removing her dress.

"Let me." Red Hawk told Emma as he reached out and grasped her trembling hand.

"The Whites are putting up some kind of structure at their old campsite." Gray Wolf said at the meeting with Red Hawk and Gold Eagle.

"What kind of building is it?" Gold Eagle asked.

"It's a fort, is what they call it, a wall of wood." Red Hawk said to answer the question for Gray Wolf.

"What should we do about it?" Gold Eagle asked as he turned back to Red Hawk.

"They are building it to make them feel safe; it is no threat to the people after all it's made of wood. If it ever becomes a threat to the tribe I'll burn it down." Red Hawk assured Gold Eagle.

Gray Wolf started to say something but new better than to question a Chief's decision. He had seen how far along the whites had come with their fort. He had also seen the power of their guns and if they put their guns behind that wall it wouldn't be easy as burning them out. Red Hawk could tell from the look on Gray Wolf's face that he didn't like what he was hearing. To Gray Wolf's credit he said nothing.

"Red Hawk, you know best how to handle these whites so I'll leave them to you." Gold Eagle told him then left.

George was helping John dig a posthole when he stopped and stared toward the village.

"Master John, will them Indians ever let my Emma come home?" He asked.

"George, Red Hawk isn't holding Emma against her will." John told him as he too stopped working.

"I'm sure now that Red Hawk is the Chief that he has been too busy to bring her home." John said.

John could see that his words hadn't taken away George's fears.

"Look George I'll go to the village tomorrow and check on Emma for you if you get back to work." John told him.

"Yes Master John." George said with a smile then began digging in the ground with a new energy.

Little Dove, Two Stars, Rose, and the baby had all been left at the cabin so James had been chosen to take Emma's place helping Liz and Ruth with the cooking. He didn't mind it too much since all he had to do was keep the fire going and fetch the water. Once that had been done he was going to sneak off and try to find Little Dove. His next problem would be getting Little Dove alone away from Rose.

Gray Wolf knew that he wasn't supposed to be spying on Two Starz's cabin anymore but he wasn't spying on Two Stars it was Little Dove he was looking for. Gray Wolf had been in love with her since he was a boy. At first it was the fact that she was four years older than him that stopped him from telling her that he was in love with her. Then there was Red Hawk her brother and Talking Bear's number one brave. Red Hawk thought that Gray Wolf was beneath his sister and told him so. Gray Wolf tried to forget about his love for her but each night she would steal his dreams. When he saw Rose come out on the cabin porch he knew that Little Dove would be close behind her.

"Is Emma going to come home today?" Rose asked as Little Dove came out behind her.

"I sure hope so." Little Dove said more to herself than to Rose. A smile crossed Little Dove's face when she heard James as he came up the creek bed. She knew it was him because no Indian would make so much noise. Before Rose could see James Little Dove placed her hand on Rose's shoulder and turned her toward her.

"I need you to help me pick some flowers for Two Stars and Spotted Bear, ok?" She asked.

Without a word Rose looked up and shook her head yes. "Good, good, you go inside and find us something to put them in." Little Dove said as she pushed Rose back toward the door.

As soon as Rose had went in the door James came into view. Gray Wolf too had heard James as he noisily made his way into the clearing. Before James could make it to the cabin Little Dave was off the porch and dragging him into the woods. James was almost as puzzled as Gray Wolf as to what was going on.

"Is there something wrong?" James asked once they had stopped. Little Dove put her arms around him and her head on his chest before she told him.

"No it's just that with Rose always around we never have time to ourselves anymore."

At first Gray Wolf thought the white boy was attacking Little Dove but as he aimed his bow toward James he saw it. There was no fight in Little Dove. Gray Wolf felt that the arrow hit his heart instead. He was tempted to go ahead and let the arrow find its mark until he saw Little Dove kissing James.

"What was that?" James asked when he heard the sound of Gray Wolf moving away from them through the underbrush.

"I don't know." She said as she too had heard the sound.

"Rose is that you?" Little Dove asked thinking Rose had found them.

They both breathed a breath of relief when Rose said yes.

"Why were you hiding in the bushes?" Little Dove asked once Rose came into view.

"I was afraid." Rose said.

"Afraid of what?" James asked.

Rose looked at them in a funny way then pointed toward the trees and said, "Indian."

Little Dove grabbed Rose by the hand and pulled her along as she hurried back toward the cabin.

Blue Bird went about her work with the other women as though she too liked Red Hawk's new woman. She acted as though her sister Two Feathers just stayed with Emma but the slave girl liked her best. Spotted Elk looked at Blue Bird and without a word told Blue Bird that she knew better. Spotted Elk's attention was taken away from Blue Bird and drawn to the white man that rode into the village. John could feel all the eyes on him as he rode toward Red Hawk's teepee.

"What do you want here?" Gray Wolf asked as John got off his horse.

"I've come to see Emma and Red Hawk." John said in a tone that told Gray Wolf he wasn't leaving until he did.

Gray Wolf pointed toward the teepee where John could find Emma. John had remembered Two Stars telling him to never show fear. He tried to hide it the best he could but he thought that all Gray Wolf had to do was look at his chest and see how hard his heart was beating. At first Two Feathers was frightened when John walked into the teepee. The fear soon left her as she remembered Emma telling her how the whites were like family to her. Two Feathers watched as a smile came to Emma's face when she heard John's voice.

"Master John!" Emma shouted as he sat down beside her.

"Emma you have no Master now that you is free." John told her as he took Emma by the hand.

"Yes I know Master John but this here is my good friend Two Feathers." Emma said pointing at the girl standing in front of him.

"Glad to meet you." John said as he rose to his feet and stuck out his hand to Two Feathers.

"My wife is Two Stars, do you know her?" He asked with a big smile on his face.

Two Feathers looked at John and wondered why he asked such a strange question.

"I know her well she is my father's sister, Talking Bear, do you know him?"

The smile left John's face and his hand fell back to his side as Two Feathers turned and left.

"How is maw, pa, and Rose?" Emma asked as John sat back down beside her.

"How are you feeling Emma?" John asked as his eyes turned toward the door that Two Feathers had just left through.

"The people here treat me good just like you all did." Rose said with a smile.

"I come to tell you that we have almost got Fort Huff ready to move into." John said in a pleasant tone.

"Oh I want to see it." Emma said with excitement in her voice.

"When it's finished I'll come and get you." John told her as he looked out the door one more time.

"Now that Red Hawk is Chief he is always gone so he will not care I'm sure." Emma told John.

"Does Rose miss me as much as I do her?" Emma asked.

John laughed then told Emma, "Rose misses you but Little Dove misses you more."

"Oh poor thing I can just see Rose holding on to Little Dove's dress like she did mine." Emma said sadly.

"I must be going now." John said as he rose to his feet.

"I will go and see Red Hawk before I leave." He told Emma as he went out the door.

John was surprised to find Two Feathers standing just a short distance from the door. He started to say something to her but from the way she looked at him he decided not to. Without a word as soon as he had passed her she quickly went back inside. After John turned back around he found Gray Wolf standing with Gold Eagle right in front of him. Even before John could greet him, Gold Eagle asked him about the fort.

"It's just a wall around the cabins that my pa built." John told him.

"And just what is the wall for?" Gray Wolf asked very loudly.

"You will come with me and tell this to Red Hawk and the others." Gold Eagle ordered.

The Idea that the Indians wouldn't like the fort hadn't crossed John's mind before now.

"This way." Gold Eagle said as he led the way while Gray Wolf walked behind John.

No one was more surprised to see John come through the door of the meeting than Red Hawk. What was more surprising was that Gold Eagle brought him there. It wasn't until Red Hawk saw the smile come to Gray Wolf's face did he speak to Gold Eagle.

"Gold Eagle it is a surprise that you would join us for such a small matter as we are talking of now." Red Hawk said as he offered a seat beside him.

Both Gray Wolf and John sat with the other braves in front of Red Hawk. Everyone fell silent as Gold Eagle began to speak.

"I have brought you this man to tell us the reason for the fort." He said as he looked at John.

Show no fear kept going through John's mind as he rose back to his feet. Red Hawk started to say something and with just one look Gold Eagle stopped him. John looked around the room before he spoke.

"We built the fort for protection of my family and my son Spotted Bear." John said without fear.

"Protect him from whom?" Gray Wolf asked loudly.

"Protect him from his own people?" Gray Wolf asked even before John could answer the first question.

"Yes from us." Red Hawk said knowing everyone there knew what Talking Bear tried to do.

Gold Eagle rose to his feet.

"Your son's protection is my job and mine alone." Gold Eagle said as he walked out.

John quickly lost his smile as he turned back to Red Hawk.

"You must tell your father to take down the walls of your fort." Red Hawk told him once he was facing him.

"But why?" John asked in a tone that Red Hawk couldn't let him get by with in front of the others.

John knew from the looks on the Indians' faces that he had messed up.

"I am sorry Chief Red Hawk it was out of my mouth that I spoke before thinking." John said as he turned his eyes toward the ground.

Red Hawk spoke loudly for all to hear.

"If you and your father take down the walls it will prove that you are one of the people."

"I will tell him but I can't say what pa is going to do about it." John told him.

Red Hawk put out a hand and placed it on John's shoulder.

"Tell him that if he is not of the people then he is the enemy of the people." Red Hawk said as he took his hand off John's shoulder.

The braves watched as John turned and walked out without a word.

Blue Bird could tell by the cool damp air and the way she could see her breath that it wouldn't be long before the snow would come. As she stood and watched Two Feathers going toward Red Hawk's teepee she let out a low grown. Two Feathers has been staying with the slave girl for so long now that she has grown close to her. As long as Two Feathers was with her Blue Bird couldn't find a way to get rid of her. She would have to find a way to do it without Red Hawk knowing that she was in on it. If he even suspected that she was involved her death wasn't going to be quick like her fathers. Blue Bird didn't know if it was the morning air or the thought of her death that caused the chill to run up her back. Not knowing which had caused it she turned around and went back inside. Red Hawk had already left by the time Two Feathers arrived. Emma was lying on the bed without moving so Two Feathers thought she was asleep. Trying to be as quiet as she could she sat down.

"I'm not asleep." Emma said just as she got seated.

"I see that Red Hawk has left early today." Two Feathers said as she looked around the teepee.

"Yes he had something to do that bothered him." Emma told her.

"Do you know what it was?" Emma asked in hopes that Two Feathers might know.

"My sister Blue Bird said that Gold Eagle told Red Hawk to get rid of the fort the whites have built." Two Feathers said with excitement in her voice.

A fear shot through Emma that was more frightening than when she lost her sight.

"Red Hawk couldn't be out to harm her people he just wouldn't do that." Emma said more to herself than to Two Feathers.

Seeing the fear that she had caused in Emma Two Feathers tried to undo the damage she had done.

"Red Hawk will just talk to them is all." Two Feathers said as she moved closer to the bed.

"The whites are Red Hawk's friends he wouldn't hurt a friend would he?" Two Feathers asked with a laugh.

"No I guess your right he wouldn't." Emma said then made herself laugh to hide her lingering fears.

"You need to get out of this teepee and meet the people of the village." Two Feathers told Emma.

"What do you mean we have got to take down the walls!?" Adam yelled when John told him what had been said at the village.

"Look pa it's not all that bad Gold Eagle just wanted us to show that we are part of the people." John told Adam.

"Do we have to live in teepees to be part of the people?" Adam asked loudly.

"Pa they didn't say a thing about the cabins." John said pointing at them.

"John we can't live in safety without them walls you know that." Adam said in a lower tone.

"At least you will be living pa." John told him.

Adam's eyes first looked at the fort walls then turned back toward where Ruth and Liz were cooking. The sound of horses brought Adam's attention back to the path leading from the creek. Red Hawk was the first one Adam saw and as each brave came into view the harder his heart pounded. He was followed by the brave called Gray Wolf and a much older Indian and five young braves. Adam wasn't the only one there who was feeling the fear as they approached them. As soon as the three got close enough Adam saw Gold Eagle stop and get down off his horse. Everyone watched as Gold Eagle looked at the walls of the fort.

"You must take down these walls." Gold Eagle told Adam as he turned back to face him.

"But why?" Adam asked once he was looking at him.

Adam saw the anger cover Gold Eagle's face then go away as fast as it had come.

"You do not know our ways so I will tell you this time." Gold Eagle told Adam loudly. "It is so Spotted Bear can see all the land that he, as Chief, must protect from our enemies."

"Gold Eagle that is why my pa built the fort is to protect Chief

Spotted Bear from our enemies." John said pointing at the walls.

Just as Gold Eagle was about to speak everyone's attention was drawn back to the creek. Two Stars sat on a horse while Little Dove led it and she was carrying Spotted Bear in her arms.

Gold Eagle turned to the east and out stretched both of his arms.

"Think you old Great Spirit for giving our people a new Chief." He said as he looked up.

As soon as Little Dove had told her that she saw the braves heading for the fort Two Stars made her bring her there. Two Stars handed Little Dove the baby so she could get off the horse. She had to take her time because she was still weak from the ride. Two Stars slowly walked over and stood by John's side before she spoke.

"What is the matter Gold Eagle?" Two Stars asked once she stood in front of him.

"I have come to take down the walls for Spotted Bear." Gold Eagle said loudly.

Without a word Two Stars turned to Little Dove and took back the baby.

"Just as Spotted Bear is of our people so is he of the people here." Two Stars said pointing at Adam.

"Just as you wish to protect Spotted Bear so do they." She said as she placed her arm back under the baby.

"Red Hawk you can take the braves back to the village." Two Stars said as she turned to him.

"It is my job to protect Spotted Bear!" Gold Eagle yelled louder than Two Stars liked.

"It was John's people that protected Spotted Bear from his own people and Talking Bear!" She yelled back not trying to hide her anger.

Gold Eagle could only look down knowing that Two Starz's words were all true. Even Gray Wolf was surprised when John stepped forward as Gold Eagle turned to leave.

"Gold Eagle to show that we are part of the people we will not put in the front wall." John said.

Adam started to say something until he saw a smile come to Gold Eagle's face. It was then that Adam decided to hold his tongue. Red Hawk looked at Gray Wolf and noticed how his eyes kept going back and forth from Little Dove and James.

"Little Dove has chosen the one she wants, it would be unwise to not honor her wish." Red Hawk said then got back on his horse.

Little Dove pretended not to notice how Gray Wolf was looking at her or the cold chill it caused her. James too had seen how he watched them.

Blue Bird couldn't believe it when she saw Two Feathers bringing Emma out into the cold air. She could tell they were talking by the way their breaths sent smoke signals through the morning air. She noticed how when they were talking the smoke was short and when they laugh the smoke seemed to go on forever. The thought of when her and Two Feathers once laughed like that only made Blue Bird more angry. Even through the cool morning air Emma could feel the sun on her face. She couldn't see it but the warmth on her face told her that it was there.

"Now you take my hand and follow me." Two Feathers said as she began pulling Emma along.

Emma was surprised how easy she found it to put her faith in Two Feathers to be her eyes. As she was being pulled along Emma noticed how they had come to a sudden stop.

"What is it?" Emma asked.

"What do you want?" Two Feathers asked as she let go of Emma's hand.

Emma wasn't sure if Two Feathers was talking to her or someone else until Blue Bird spoke.

"Oh I just came to say hello to Red Hawk's woman." Blue Bird said as she waved a hand in front of Emma's eyes.

Two Feathers knew that Emma couldn't see a thing or she wouldn't have a smile on her face.

"Well think you." Emma was saying when Two Feathers started pulling on her again.

"What is your hurry sister?" Blue Bird said as she took Emma's other arm and began pulling Emma in the other direction.

Both the dirt and dried grass had a light frost on them and Emma's feet had no traction. When she jerked her arms hard to get them free of the two girl's grip she lost her balance and fell. Emma's head hit hard on the ground and the blow burst open her head wound and the blood began flowing in a stream on the ground. Both Blue Bird and Two Feathers stared in shock at Emma lying in a pool of blood on the ground.

"What are we going to do?" Blue Bird asked when she found her voice.

"Go get some help." Two Feathers said not seeing the crowd that had begun to reach them.

As soon as Blue Bird saw them she yelled loud enough for all to hear her I'll get help then took off in a run. All the way to the teepee Blue Bird's thoughts were on how Red Hawk was going kill her. She never stopped running until she was safely inside. Blue Bird wasn't the only one that feared for her life Two Feathers to thought her life was over. Two Feathers watched as a few of the braves lifted Emma off the ground and packed her home. Two Feathers thought Emma looked dead as they packed her away.

"As soon as Red Hawk finds out what happened I will end up as dead as her." Two Feathers said.

She took both hands and wiped the tears from her eyes. Two Feathers didn't know if the tears were for herself or her new friend as she started following the men ahead of her. As she stood waiting for the braves to get Emma inside her teepee Two Feathers saw Red Hawk and the others returning.

As soon as Red Hawk saw the crowd around his teepee he knew there was something wrong there. He jumped down and ran toward them.

With just a glance at Two Feathers as he went by her, he told her, "I will be back."

The only way Red Hawk could tell that Emma wasn't dead was by her breaths she took. Seeing that Emma was being cared for Red Hawk's anger drove him back outside and Two Feathers. He was glad to see Gray Wolf standing there as he came out. Before saying a word to Two Feathers he ordered Gray Wolf to go and bring Little Dove to him. Two Feathers was shaking all over by the time Red Hawk turned to her. Seeing how frightened Two Feathers was of him Red Hawk tried to hide his anger from her.

"What happened?" Red Hawk asked as low as he could.

"I don't know we were just going for a walk and then Blue Bird started pulling on her arm and she fell." Two Feathers said pointing toward where it happened.

Red Hawk's anger returned with a vengeance when he heard Blue Bird's name.

"Where is she!" He yelled as he grabbed Two Feathers by the arm.

"I don't know Red Hawk she just ran off."

Two Feathers seen the anger as Red Hawk let go of her arm and stormed off toward her teepee.

John and James helped Little Dove get Two Stars back to the cabin so she could rest.

As soon as Two Stars lied down and Little Dove placed Spotted Bear in her arms she fell asleep. James and Little Dove stood just outside the door talking about something that he decided was not his problem. So instead of going out to join them he sat down beside Spotted Bear and Two Stars and watched them from a distance.

"What is wrong with you?" Little Dove asked as James paced back and forth in front of her.

"I don't know how to say this. I really don't know if I have the right to ask this but I have to know, did you and Gray Wolf... you know... like us?" James asked.

It took all of Little Dove's power not to laugh in James's face but she heard his fear in his question. Little Dove placed her arms around James and pulled him closer to her. She waited until their lips were almost touching before she said anything.

"No." She said as she pressed her lips to his.

The sound of Gray Wolf's horse was what broke the kiss.

"Red Hawk sent me to get you so get your things and lets go." Gray Wolf ordered.

Little Dove didn't know what angered her the most the fact that Red Hawk had sent Gray Wolf for her or that Gray Wolf was ordering her.

"You tell my brother that I will come when I get ready." Little Dove told Gray Wolf.

Gray Wolf stared at James in silence before he spoke again.

"It's the slave girl." Gray Wolf said then watched James's reaction.

John came out just in time to hear the part about the slave girl.

"What about the slave girl?!" John yelled as he reached Little Dove's side. Being that John was the father of Spotted Bear Gray Wolf had to answer him.

"She fell and needs Little Dove's help right now." Gray Wolf said then turned his horse and rode off not bothering to look behind him.

"I'll get my things and go with you." John said as he turned to go back inside.

"No." Little Dove said loudly stopping John in his tracts.

"You must stay here with Two Stars; James can come with me."

Blue Bird wet herself when Red Hawk came in her teepee without being asked.

"What did you do to my woman?!" Red Hawk yelled once he was in front of her.

"I did nothing to her Red Hawk she just slipped and fell I swear." Blue Bird said as she leaned back as much as she could.

If Red Hawk could prove that Blue Bird wasn't telling the truth he would cast her out of the village right now.

"If I find that you have lied to me you will regret the day you were born!" Red Hawk yelled at her before turning and walking out.

It was a long time after Red Hawk had left before Blue Bird could move. As she sat staring at the door and hearing her heart pound in her ears she wondered if her father had felt this fear in his last breath. Two

Feathers waited until Red Hawk had left before she went inside to see if Red Hawk had killed her sister. Blue Bird told herself that seeing that the slave girl was dead by now Red Hawk couldn't find out the truth about what happened. A cold chill run up her back as Two Feathers entered.

"I told Red Hawk that the slave girl slipped and fell is how she died." Blue Bird said as she jumped to her feet.

"You must tell him the same story or he will kill me." Blue Bird pleaded as she grabbed Two Feathers by the arms.

Two Feathers jerked her arms free of Blue Bird's grip and stepped back.

"The slave girl isn't dead is what I heard and I'm not going to lie to Chief Red Hawk and die for it."

"It wasn't my idea to take her for a walk in the frost." Blue Bird said as she retook Two Feathers by the arms.

"Just remember sister if he kills me you will be next on his list!" Blue Bird yelled as she jerked her hands away from Two Feathers.

Two Feathers heart was pounding so hard as Blue Bird Walked out she could hear it in her ears. In a panic Two Feathers ran out the door straight into Little Dove heading toward Red Hawk's teepee. Little Dove didn't give Two Feathers a glance as she brushed past her heading for the door. One look from Red Hawk as Two Feathers came into the teepee told her that she wasn't welcome.

"Get everyone out of here except you." Little Dove ordered as she pointed toward the maiden she had left in charge while she was gone.

"That goes for you too Red Hawk." Little Dove said as she turned to him.

Red Hawk waited until the rest were gone before he too walked out without a word. Red Hawk found Gray Wolf standing beside James at the horses. They both took their eyes off each other and turned them to Red Hawk as he walked up.

"Gray Wolf you will find Blue Bird and Two Feathers and see they do not leave their teepee." Red Hawk ordered.

With just a glance back at James Gray Wolf walked away without saying a thing.

"Little Dove told me to wait here." James said as Red Hawk turned to him.

Red Hawk couldn't understand what his sister saw in this boy. There was one thing he knew that he didn't want to know.

"Then that's what you should do." Red Hawk said over his shoulder as he walked off.

"Can I wait with you Red Hawk?" James asked.

As soon as Little Dove started washing Emma's face with a wet cloth she opened her eyes.

What she did next surprised Little Dove even more. Emma brought her hand up to her eyes to block them from the sun light. After Little Dove got over the shock she gently pushed Emma's hand down and placed the wet cloth on her eyes instead.

"Go tell the boy at the horses to come here then find Red Hawk and tell him the same thing." Little Dove ordered her helper.

"Don't." Emma said as she pushed Little Dove's hand away taking the cloth with it.

Emma's life had been spent in darkness for months now she craved the darkness to shut off the light. Emma cried out as pain shot through both her eyes making her bring her arm back to cover them again. The sound of Red Hawk's voice was what made Emma try seeing again.

Emma was just as shocked as Red Hawk when she sat up in bed and saw him at her side.

"Master James." Emma said when she saw him standing behind Red Hawk.

Emma realized that her price for freedom would cost her dearly.